TALES OF THE DEAD

ANCIENT EGYPT

Written by Stuart Ross
Consultant Dr. Joann Fletcher
Illustrated by Inklink & Richard Bonson

DK

LONDON, NEW YORK, MUNICH,
MELBOURNE, and DELHI

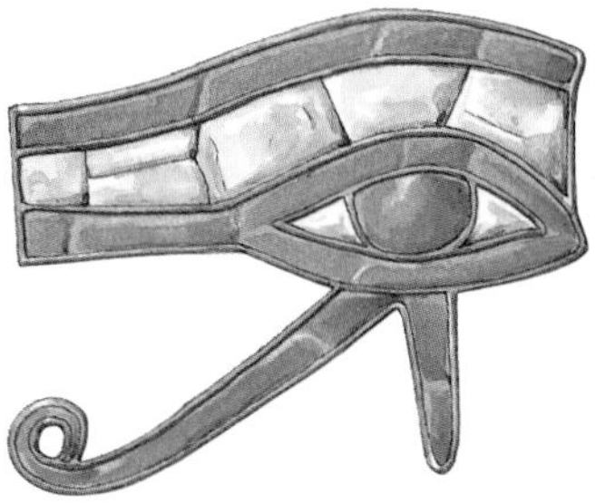

SENIOR EDITOR Simon Beecroft
ART EDITOR/STORY VISUALIZER John Kelly
ART DIRECTOR Mark Richards
PUBLISHING MANAGER Cynthia O'Neill Collins
PUBLISHER Alex Kirkham
PRODUCTION Jenny Jacoby
US EDITOR Christine Heilman
DTP DESIGNER Eric Shapland

First American Edition, 2003

Published in the United States by
DK Publishing, Inc.
375 Hudson Street
New York, New York 10014

03 04 05 06 07 08 10 9 8 7 6 5 4 3 2 1

A Cataloging-in-Publication record for this book is available from the Library of Congress.

ISBN 0-7894-9857-X

Color reproduction by Media Development and Printing Ltd
Printed and bound in Italy by L.E.G.O.

Discover more at
www.dk.com

ACKNOWLEDGMENTS

Richard Bonson painted the town (p.6-7), Egyptian society (p.8-9), pyramids (p.10-11), pyramid interior (p.12-13), house of the dead (p.16-17), temple of Sobek (p.18-19), and large boat (p.22).

All other artworks, including graphic novel, painted by Inklink.

The author would like to thank the pupils of King Ethelbert's School, Birchington; Dulwich College Prep School, Coursehorn; Finham Park School, Coventry; and North Curry Primary School, Somerset, for their valuable input in the preparation of this book.

Contents

6 Town Life

8 Egyptian Society

10 Tombs for the Gods

12 Into the Pyramid

14 Making Mummies

16 House of the Dead

18 Temple of Sobek

20 The River of Life

22 On the Nile

24 The Great House

26 Keeping the Peace

28 Craftworking

30 Facing the Gods

32 Index

Stone tablet carved with hieroglyphs (picture writing)

It is early morning in Egypt and the air is alive with sounds: the shouts of sailors in their boats, the clutter of shopkeepers laying out their wares, the steady creak of plows being driven through the fields...

A scribe

The dusty streets are busy with shaven-headed people. A wealthy official in white linen glides by, his jewelry glinting in the sun. From the desert sands rise gleaming pyramids and monuments, while deep within brightly painted temples inscribed with a mysterious picture writing, sneering statues of terrifying gods stare, unblinking.

Servants attending to noblewomen

This is Egypt 4,000 years ago, when its mighty civilization was at its height. For three millennia, the ancient Egyptians flourished along the banks of the Nile River, transforming the dry desert into a land of wonders. Finally, attacked from north and south, during the first millennium CE this glorious civilization gradually crumbled away...

Female musicians

The many buildings, pictures, objects and texts tell us a great deal about life in ancient Egypt. Using this wealth of treasures, we have brought the amazing Egyptians back to life in these pages. Here you will meet royalty, courtiers, scribes, priests, servants, and tomb-robbers, and hear the tales of ordinary people, long dead. Just watch out for the sinister snap of the crocodile—and beware the Curse of Sobek!

TIMELINE

1969
US astronauts land on the Moon

1492
Columbus sails to America

1206
Genghis Khan conquers Asia

410
Roman Empire collapsing

44 BCE
Death of Julius Caesar

PRESENT DAY

2000 CE   1000 CE   0 CE

THE CURSE OF THE CROCODILE GOD

The story takes place in the year 1795 BCE during the reign of the female pharaoh Sobekneferu. Methen lives in a town near Hawara in the Fayum region of Lower (northern) Egypt. Look out for the many details of ancient Egyptian life on every page, from clothing and hairstyles to buildings and everyday objects.

STORY CONTINUES ON NEXT PAGE

I NEVER EVEN WANTED TO GO.
FATHER MADE ME.
IT IS THE WISH OF LORD INI TO MEET YOU, METHEN.

"MY NAME IS METHEN, and this is my friend Madja. Our lives are in great danger! We are entangled in a fiendish plot hatched by a corrupt official. As the son of a respected priest, nothing in my life has prepared me for this. My days have been spent at scribe school, learning to read and write hieroglyphics. Madja is a humble serving girl in a nobleman's court. Like me, she is thirteen years old, but our paths had never crossed... until the evening of the banquet at Lord Ini's palace.

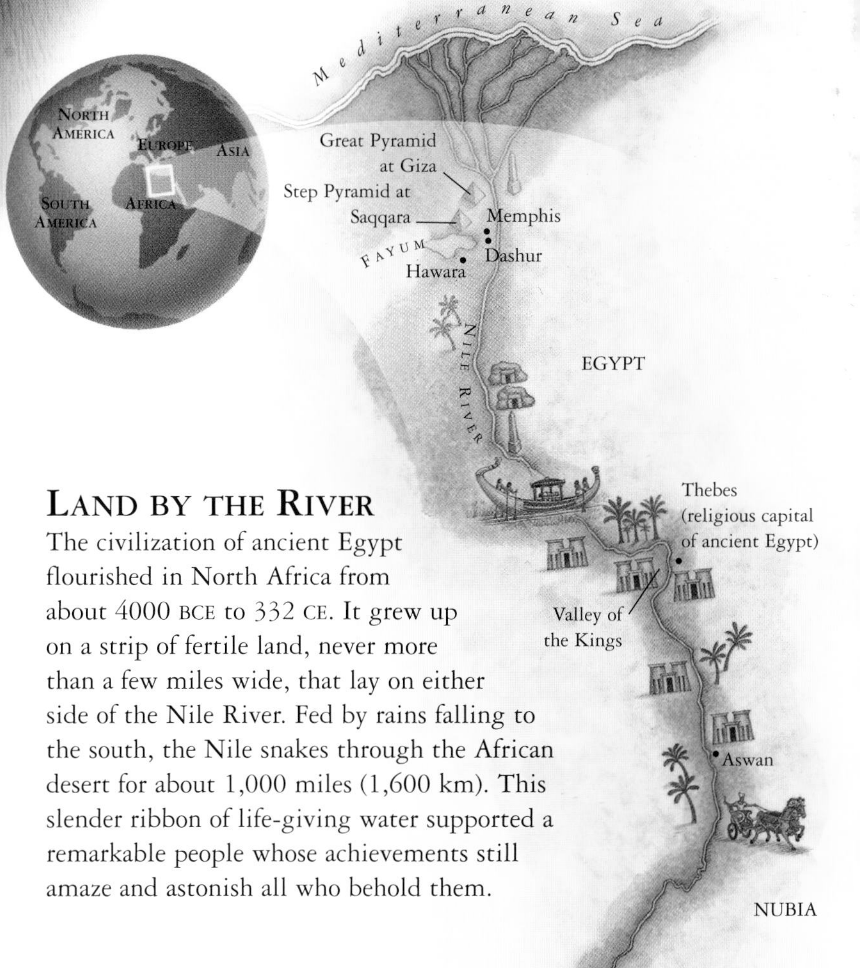

LAND BY THE RIVER

The civilization of ancient Egypt flourished in North Africa from about 4000 BCE to 332 CE. It grew up on a strip of fertile land, never more than a few miles wide, that lay on either side of the Nile River. Fed by rains falling to the south, the Nile snakes through the African desert for about 1,000 miles (1,600 km). This slender ribbon of life-giving water supported a remarkable people whose achievements still amaze and astonish all who behold them.

1153
Death of Rameses III, the last great pharaoh

*c.*1799
Sobekneferu comes to the throne.

*c.*2050
Montuhotep II reunites Egypt after years of turmoil

*c.*2585
Building of the Great Pyramid at Giza begins

3100
King Menes unites Egypt

1000 BCE — 2000 BCE — 3000 BCE

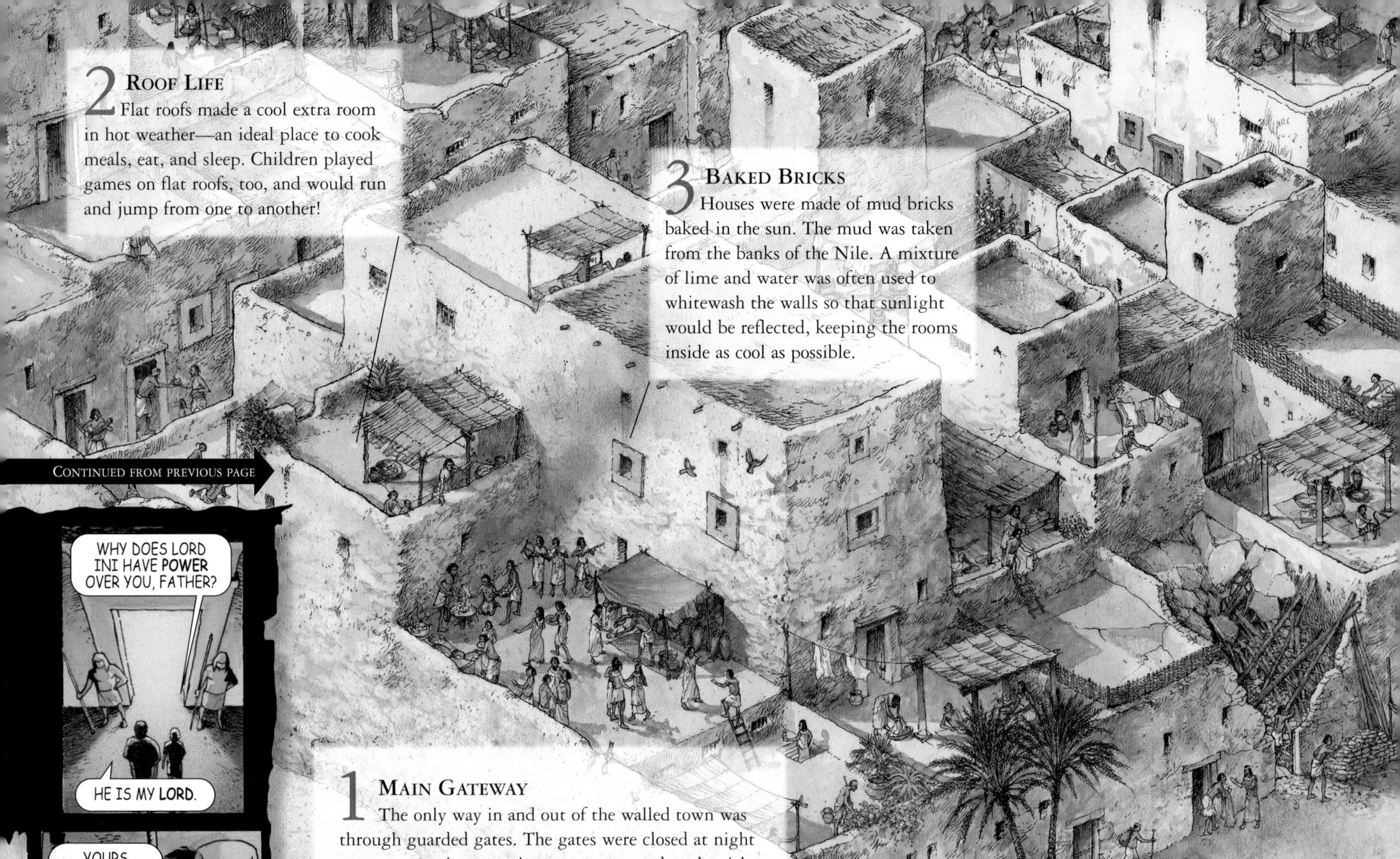

2 Roof Life
Flat roofs made a cool extra room in hot weather—an ideal place to cook meals, eat, and sleep. Children played games on flat roofs, too, and would run and jump from one to another!

3 Baked Bricks
Houses were made of mud bricks baked in the sun. The mud was taken from the banks of the Nile. A mixture of lime and water was often used to whitewash the walls so that sunlight would be reflected, keeping the rooms inside as cool as possible.

1 Main Gateway
The only way in and out of the walled town was through guarded gates. The gates were closed at night to protect against roaming gangs attracted to the rich settlements of the Nile valley.

Continued from previous page

WHY DOES LORD INI HAVE POWER OVER YOU, FATHER?
HE IS MY LORD.
YOURS TOO, METHEN.
AND THE OVERSEER OF ALL THE PRIESTS IN THE SOBEK TEMPLE.
HE IS ALSO CLOSE TO PHARAOH SOBEKNEFERU.
I'D BETTER WATCH WHAT I SAY.

Town Life

Methen and Madja live in the same town, although their lives are worlds apart. Like many towns in ancient Egypt, theirs is surrounded by high walls, like a giant fort, and its houses are crammed together in unplanned streets. The Egyptians also built large planned towns beside their great building projects, such as pyramids or temples, where thousands of workers lived.

I WILL TAKE YOU TO HIM NOW.
WE CROSSED THE CROWDED ROOM.
THEN I SAW HIM...
MY LORD AND MASTER.
LORD INI.
WELCOME, MY FRIENDS.
MY SON—METHEN.
FATHER, WHO IS THAT MAN WITH LORD INI?
SHH! QUIET.

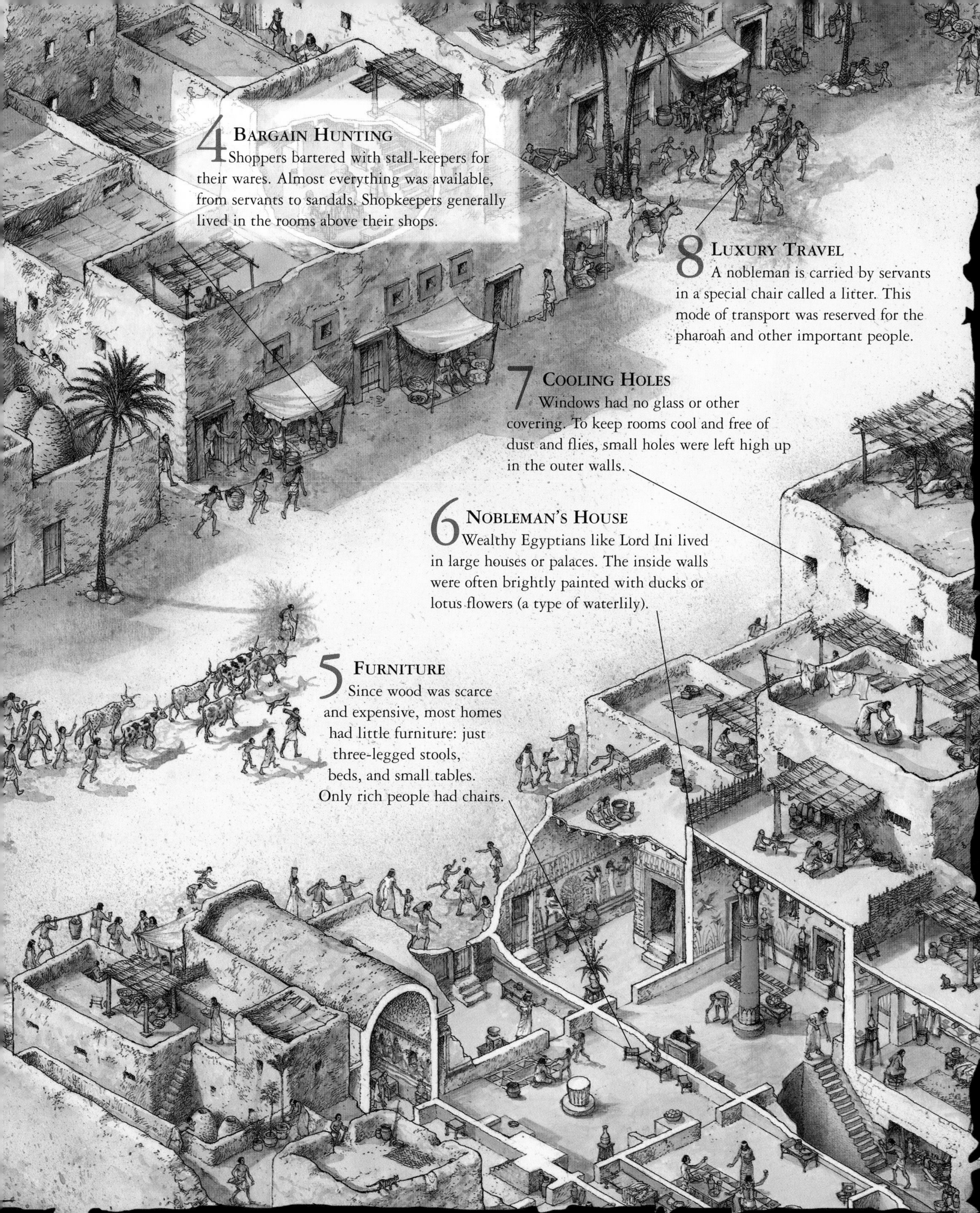

4 Bargain Hunting
Shoppers bartered with stall-keepers for their wares. Almost everything was available, from servants to sandals. Shopkeepers generally lived in the rooms above their shops.

5 Furniture
Since wood was scarce and expensive, most homes had little furniture: just three-legged stools, beds, and small tables. Only rich people had chairs.

6 Nobleman's House
Wealthy Egyptians like Lord Ini lived in large houses or palaces. The inside walls were often brightly painted with ducks or lotus flowers (a type of waterlily).

7 Cooling Holes
Windows had no glass or other covering. To keep rooms cool and free of dust and flies, small holes were left high up in the outer walls.

8 Luxury Travel
A nobleman is carried by servants in a special chair called a litter. This mode of transport was reserved for the pharoah and other important people.

Story continues on next page

HE TOLD ME IT WAS **KENAMUN**, THE CHIEF EMBALMER.
HE WAS SO **UGLY**.
I WATCHED HIM SLIDE INTO THE **SHADOWS**.
HE MET SOMEONE...
...A **SERVING** GIRL.
SHE LOOKED **TERRIFIED**.
SHE SAW ME WATCHING...
...AND HEADED **TOWARD** ME.
C...CAN I **HELP** YOU, SIR?

WHAT WERE YOU SAYING TO THAT **SERVANT**, METHEN?
NOTHING.
THE **WELL**, BY THE **KITCHEN GATE**.
CAN YOU MEET ME **TOMORROW**, AFTER SUNSET?
WHERE?
CAN **I** HELP **YOU**?
I CANNOT TALK NOW.

CONTINUED FROM PREVIOUS PAGE

THE NEXT EVENING, I CREPT OUT...
SHE WAS WAITING FOR ME.
PSST! IN HERE!

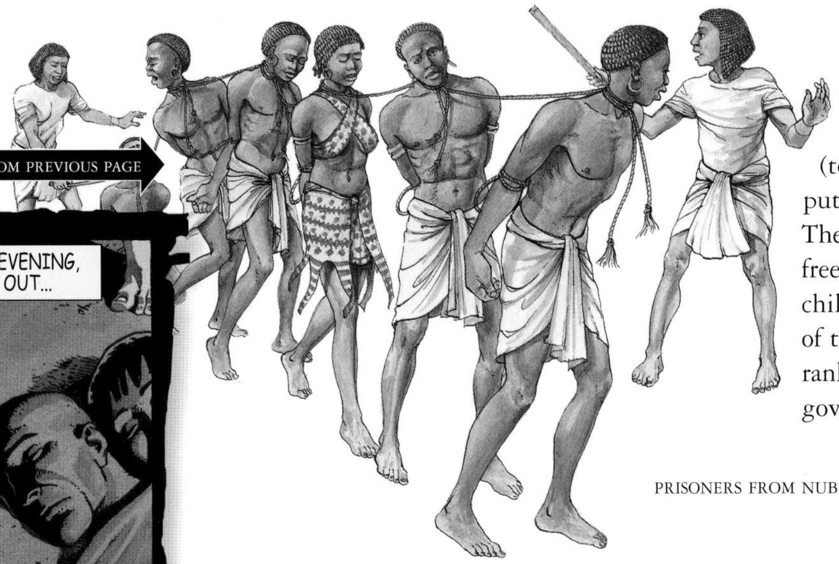

PRISONERS FROM NUBIA

PRISONERS

Prisoners brought to Egypt during its conquests in Nubia (to the south) and the Near East were put to work, often in royal workshops. These workers could obtain their own freedom or the freedom of their children. Sometimes the descendants of these prisoners attained high-ranking positions in the Egyptian government or in the military.

SERVANT

FAN BEARER

EGYPTIAN SOCIETY

Everyone knew their place in ancient Egyptian society. At the top was the king, or pharaoh, who was considered a son of the gods. On the next rung were his family, his wives and children. Below them came the top government officials, generals and priests—they were equally important because religion and politics overlapped. After the petty officials and officers came the ordinary people, farmers and laborers. Servants like Madja worked for wealthy people.

WORKER'S FAMILY

WORKERS

Ordinary men and women worked in the fields and on the pharaoh's building projects—such as when he or she ordered a pyramid-tomb or rock-cut tomb to be built. Money didn't exist in ancient Egypt, so workers were paid in food and goods.

SONG AND DANCE

No feast was complete without a troupe of musicians, acrobats, and dancers. Some performers were well respected and earned their own money working at official functions.

ACROBAT

DRESSER

MUSICIAN

SINGER

THANK YOU FOR COMING. MY NAME IS MADJA.
I AM METHEN.
YES, I ASKED OF YOU AT LORD INI'S PALACE.
YOU DID? WELL, ER, WHAT IS YOUR TROUBLE?
IT IS NOT EASY TO SPEAK ABOUT. I - AM - BEING - FORCED INTO MARRIAGE.
TO WHOM WILL YOU BE GIVEN?
LAST NIGHT YOU SAW HIM ...
BY SOBEK'S HOLY CLAWS! NOT THAT SNAKE, KENAMUN??!!
IT CAN'T BE SO!
THE VERY MAN. I AM TO SHARE THE HOUSE OF THE CHIEF EMBALMER.
THE MAN WHOSE HANDS PULL OUT THE ENTRAILS OF THE DEAD BY DAY...

BRIDE AND GROOM

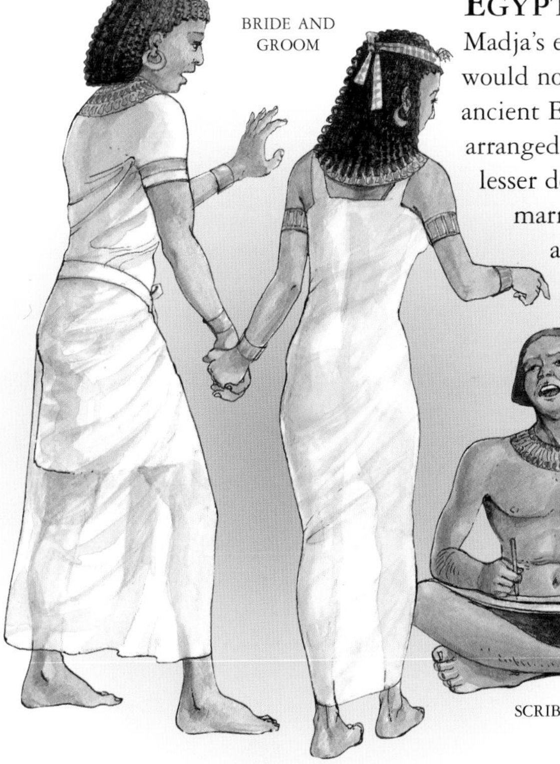

Egyptian Marriage

Madja's enforced choice of husband would not have been unusual in ancient Egypt. Most marriages were arranged by the girl's father and, to a lesser degree, mother. Girls would marry at around 13 years of age and boys at 16. A scribe could draw up a contract giving equal rights to both husband and wife. Producing children was the main purpose of marriage, and couples used all kinds of potions, prayers, and spells to get the gods to bless them with offspring. Childless couples often divorced.

SCRIBE

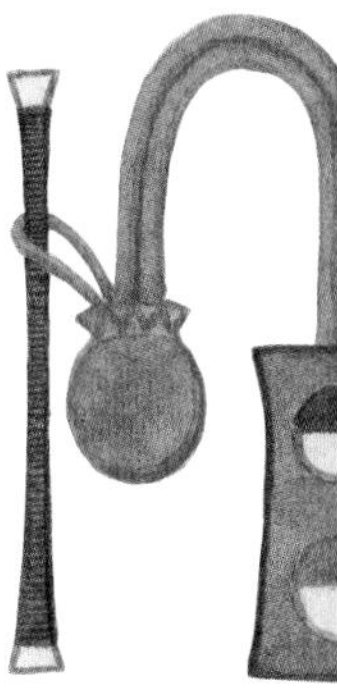

HIEROGLYPH FOR "SCRIBE"

The Army

Egypt's army fought off invaders and captured slaves. Soldiers were ordinary laborers ordered into the army by the king. They carried swords, javelins, and daggers, but wore little armor.

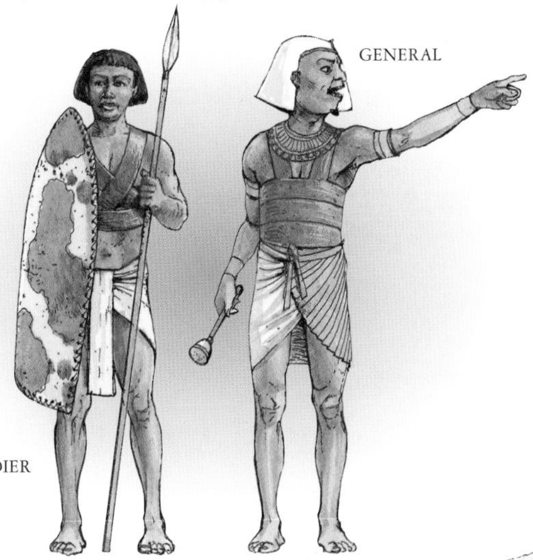

SOLDIER

GENERAL

Priests

Methen is one of the few people in ancient Egypt to learn the complicated picture writing known as hieroglyphs. He will become an official writer (called a scribe), and, eventually, a priest, like his father. Kenamun's role as Chief Embalmer is to preside over the ceremonies for preserving the dead—known as mummification. He wears a jackal mask that symbolizes Anubis, the god of the dead and mummification.

PRIEST

CHIEF EMBALMER

MINISTER

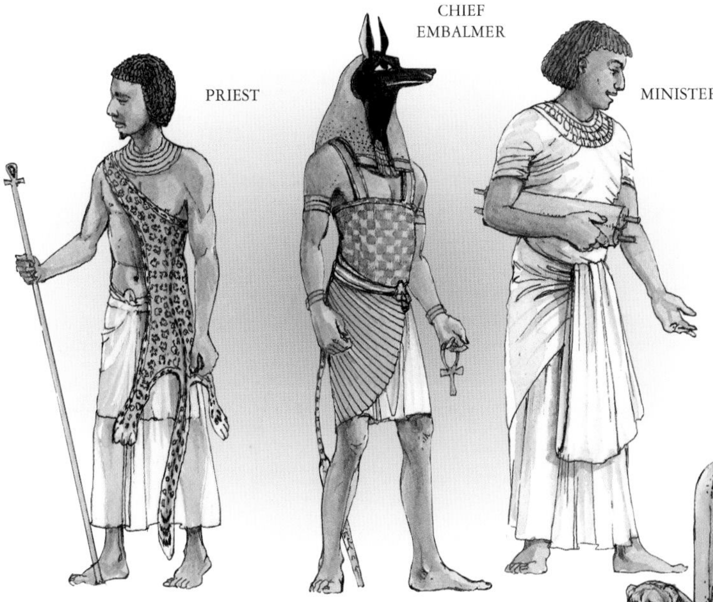

PHARAOH HATSHEPSUT

PHARAOH AND FAMILY

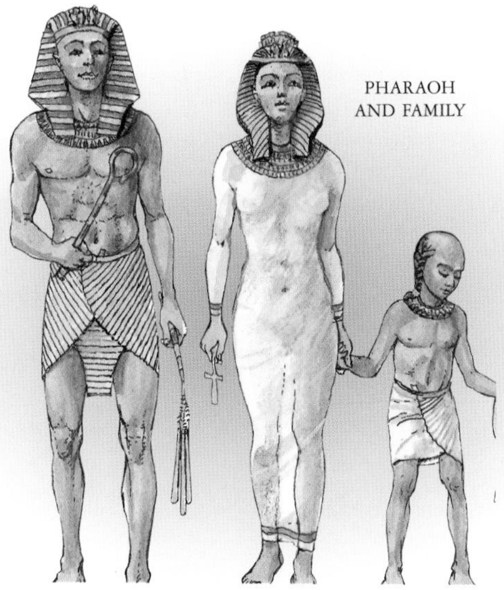

The Royal Family

The Egyptians believed that their kings, or pharaohs, were semi-gods, and therefore above the normal rules of society. Most pharaohs were men, but a handful of women ruled Egypt at several times. One of the most powerful and longest reigning female pharaohs was Hatshepsut, who ruled for about 15 years, until her death in 1458 BCE. To help her to fit in, she dressed in the traditional clothing of male rulers, and even wore a false beard!

Story continues on next page

HE HAS YEARS ENOUGH TO BE MY GRANDFATHER, AND HE OWNS A WIFE AND THREE MISTRESSES ALREADY...
SHHH!
WHO IS IT?
ONE MOMENT...
...IT'S HIM!
KENAMUN!

Tombs for the Gods

The pyramids are the most impressive of all ancient Egyptian monuments. These burial tombs for the king-gods, the pharaohs, and their queens originally stood at the heart of a complex of funeral monuments and buildings. Raised between 2686 and 1550 BCE, it was some time before the "true" pyramid shape emerged.

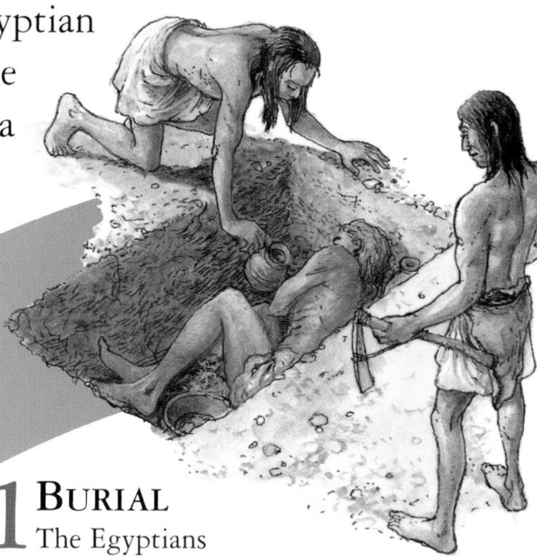

1 Burial

The Egyptians originally buried their dead in simple graves dug in the sand.

Pottery vase

2 Reed Coffin

Wood was rare, so the first coffins were woven out of reeds.

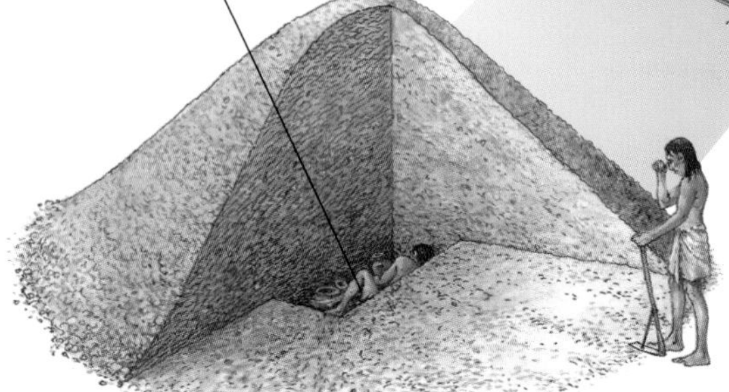

Burial pit beneath mound

3 Mound Grave

By 4,000 BCE, important graves were marked by mounds. Bodies were buried with objects they might need in the next life.

A chapel and a statue of the tomb owner lay inside.

4 Mastaba Tomb

Mastabas (from the Arabic word for "bench") were rectangular tombs for royal burials *c.*3100–2686 BCE. They then began to be used for nonroyal burials. The burial chamber was built underground, often carved from rock. The visible part—the actual bench-shaped mastaba—was built on top from brick or stone.

Burial chambers were built deep underground.

5 Step Pyramid, Saqqara

The first pyramid was built by the gifted architect Imhotep for Pharaoh Djoser (2667–2648 BCE) at Saqqara. The six-step pyramid was 200 feet (60 meters) high, and represented a staircase to the sun-god. It was made of 11.7 million cubic feet (330,400 cubic meters) of stone and clay—enough to fill 120 Olympic-size swimming pools!

Continued from previous page

KENAMUN AND TWO OTHER MEN PASSED BY US.
THEY CREPT OFF INTO THE MOONLIGHT.
WHAT ARE THEY UP TO?
THEY WERE HEADING TOWARD THE PYRAMID.
I NOTICED THAT ONE OF THE MEN HAD A LIMP.
ALL THREE CARRIED WOODEN LEVERS.

WE FOLLOWED THEM, KEEPING OUR DISTANCE.
THEY BEGAN TO CLIMB UP THE PYRAMID!

WHAT IN THE NAME OF RA?!
METHEN, BE QUIET!
USING THE LEVERS, THE MEN PRIED ASIDE A HUGE STONE.
THEY VANISHED INTO THE PYRAMID!
TOMB ROBBERS!
LET'S FOLLOW!

6 Bent Pyramid, Dashur

Pharaoh Sneferu (2613–2589 BCE) built three pyramids in an attempt to construct a true pyramid with sloping sides. He began one of the two at Dashur, with tombs inside, but the structure started to collapse before it was finished. To stop it from giving way completely, the top was finished at a different angle from the base—producing the Bent Pyramid. His third pyramid at Dashur became the first true pyramid.

7 The Great Pyramid, Giza

The reign of Pharaoh Khufu (2589-2566 BCE) saw the construction of the impressive Great Pyramid at Giza—the largest pyramid ever built.

MADJA, LOOK!
IT WAS A SECRET PASSAGEWAY LEADING INTO THE PYRAMID....

STORY CONTINUES ON NEXT PAGE

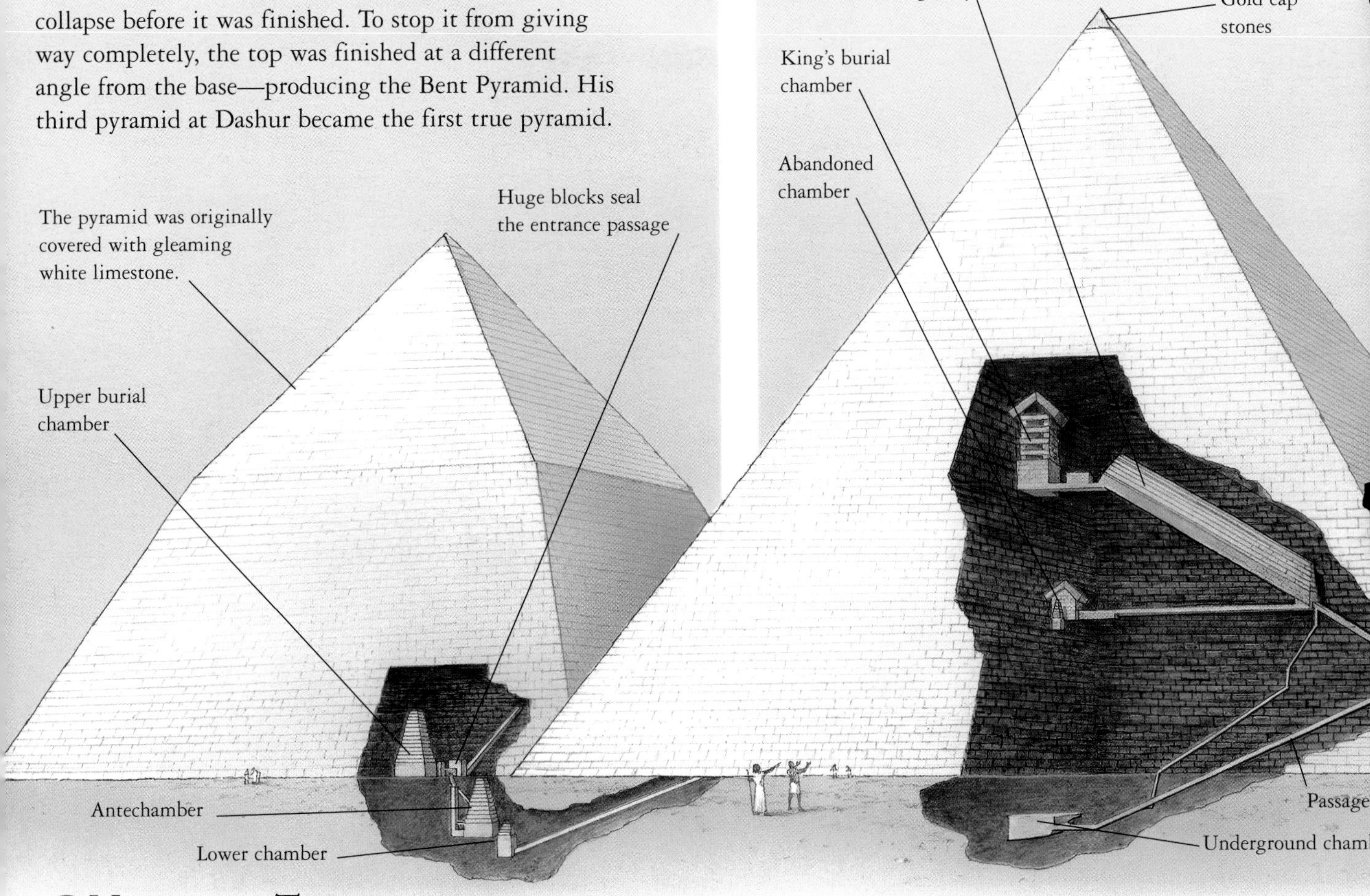

The pyramid was originally covered with gleaming white limestone.
Huge blocks seal the entrance passage
Upper burial chamber
Antechamber
Lower chamber
Grand entrance gallery
Gold cap stones
King's burial chamber
Abandoned chamber
Passageway
Secret entrance
Underground chamber

8 Mortuary Temple

Pyramids were part of a funerary complex in which a member of the royal family was laid to rest and worshiped as a god. Worship took place in a mortuary temple built near the pyramid. Its focus was a statue of the king-god, tended by priests day and night.

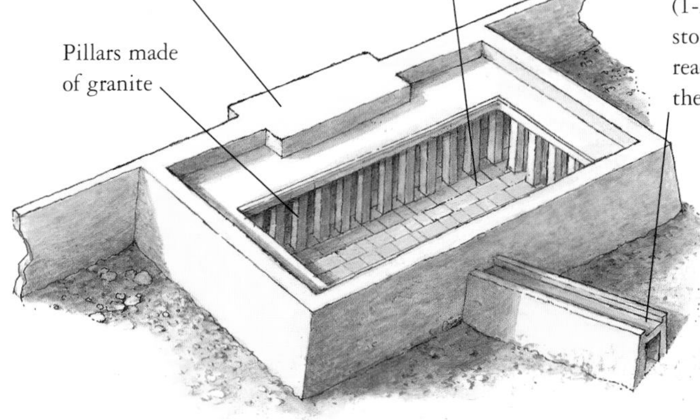

Inner rooms
Open courtyard
Pillars made of granite
A 0.6-mile-(1-kilometer) -long stone causeway reached toward the Nile

9 Rock Tombs

Pyramids might be impressive, but they were an obvious target for tomb robbers. During the New Kingdom (1550-1069 BCE), kings and other royalty were buried in tombs cut out of solid rock. Rock tombs, like the one built for King Tutankhamun and his treasure in the Valley of the Kings, were thought to be more secure.

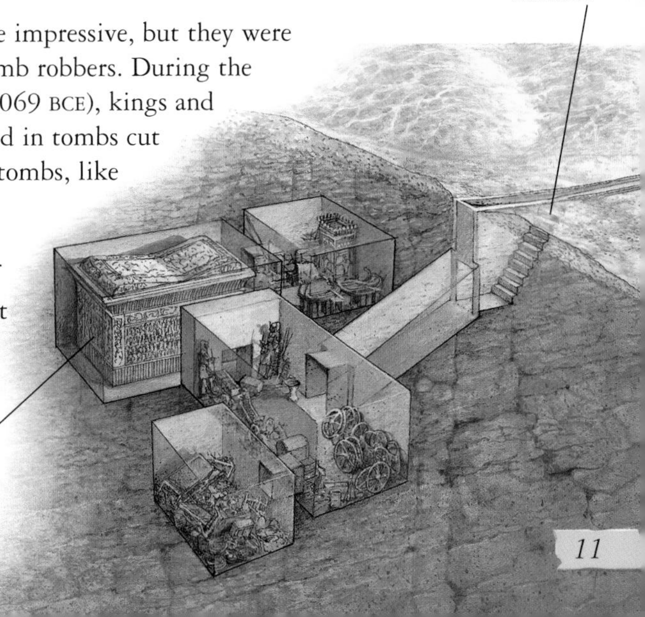

Entrance
Tutankhamun's gold shrine was so large it nearly filled one whole room of his tomb

Into The Pyramid

Ancient Egyptian pharaohs oversaw the construction of a pyramid during their lifetime so it was ready when they died. Each pyramid was different, reflecting individual taste and wealth. The body was accompanied by valuable treasures, so the temptation to rob a royal tomb was almost irresistible. But, as Methen knows, the penalty was death.

Secret Door

The entrance to a pyramid shaft was normally on the north side. It was carefully disguised with the same brick or stone as the rest of the construction. However, many people had helped build the pyramid and then witnessed the royal funeral, so the doorway was not exactly a secret.

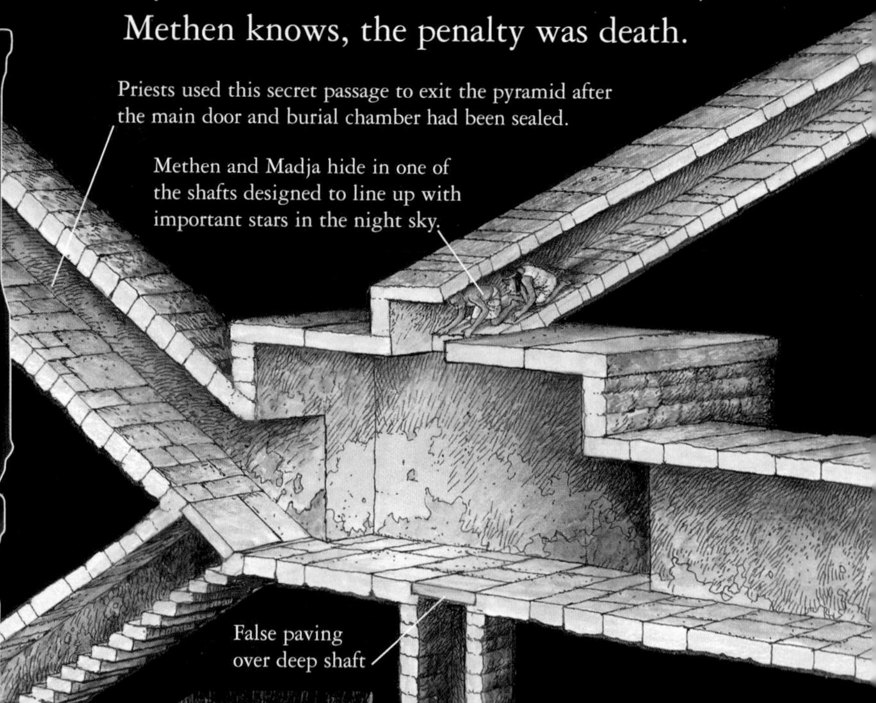

Priests used this secret passage to exit the pyramid after the main door and burial chamber had been sealed.
Methen and Madja hide in one of the shafts designed to line up with important stars in the night sky.
False paving over deep shaft

LISTEN... SOMEONE APPROACHES!
QUICKLY! UP HERE...
DON'T MOVE!

THE PASSAGEWAY WAS DARK AND HOT.
THE AIR WAS STALE.
False burial chamber to confuse robbers

IT WAS KENAMUN!

Continued from previous page

Headbanging

One way to keep out tomb robbers was to wedge heavy stone blocks above the entrance shaft. When these blocks were disturbed (for example, by opening a door), they fell down and buried the intruder.

Trapdoor

Tomb robbers had to watch their footsteps. To catch the unwary, pyramid builders laid false paving over deep shafts. When the robber stepped on the thin cover, it gave way, and he fell headlong into a dark prison— which soon became his grave.

HE WAS CARRYING A SACK.
LET US SEE WHERE THEY HAVE BEEN.
WE SAW A LIGHT AHEAD.
IT'S THE BURIAL CHAMBER!

Tunneling Down

Often, the entrance to a burial chamber was sealed with massive slabs of stone. Unable to move them, cunning robbers found a way in by removing the ceiling bricks and jumping down from above.

Story continues on next page

WE'RE TRAPPED. BURIED ALIVE!
IT WON'T MOVE!
THE ENTRANCE STONE HAS BEEN PUT BACK INTO PLACE!
THEN IT GOT WORSE.
TERRIFIED, WE RETRACED OUR STEPS.
WE MUST LEAVE.

Burial Chamber

The mummified body of the dead king was laid in the burial chamber at the heart of the pyramid. The chamber was built from granite blocks for greater strength and was shaped like a little house. Everything the deceased might need in the afterlife was packed in it, including jewelry, food and even instructions on how to make sure they made it to eternal happiness.

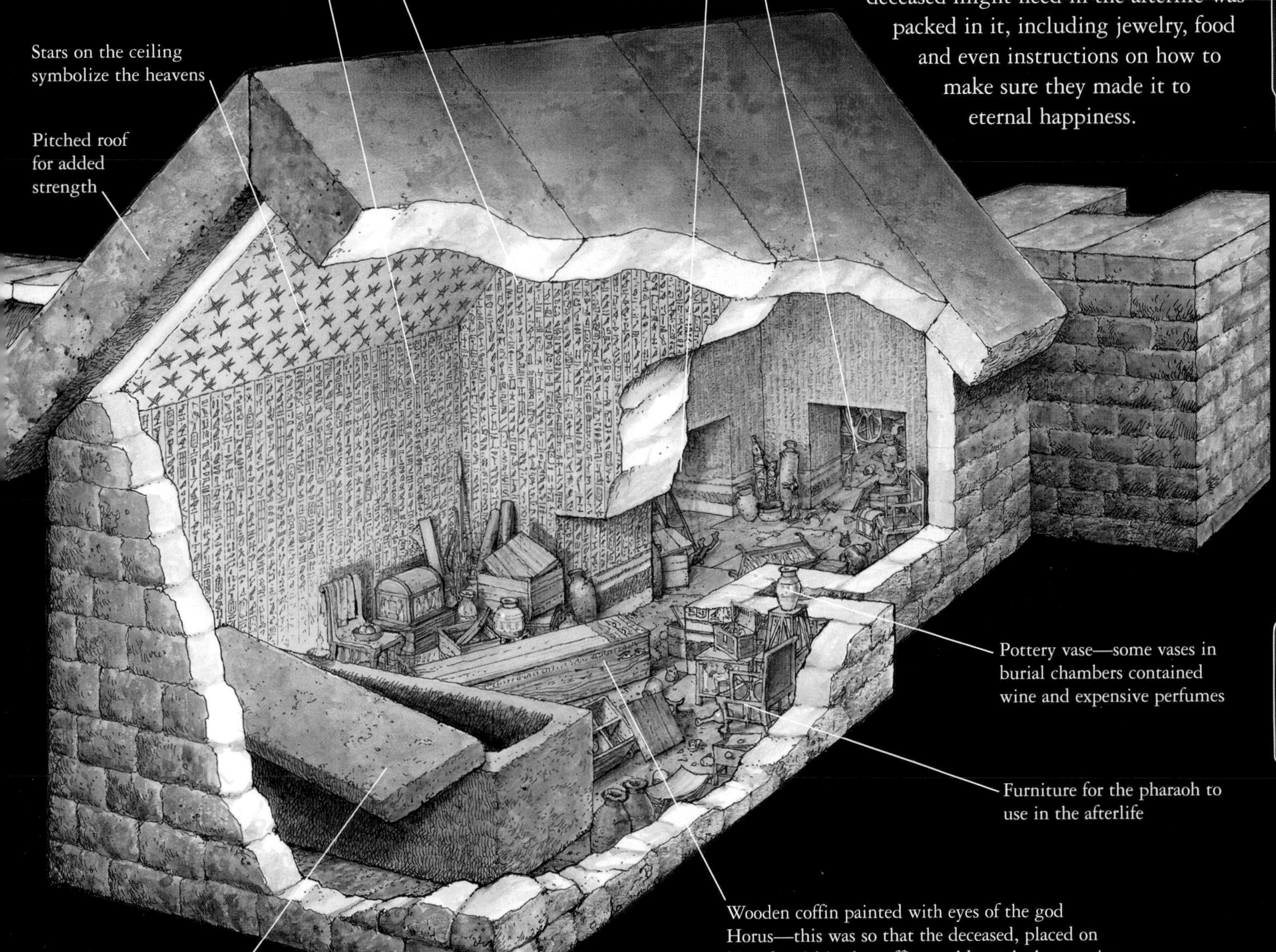

CONTINUED FROM PREVIOUS PAGE

WE PUSHED AS HARD AS WE COULD.
BUT THE STONE WOULD NOT MOVE.
WE MUST FIND SOMETHING TO PUSH IT OPEN WITH.
AT THE DOOR TO THE BURIAL CHAMBER, WE STOPPED.
THE CURSE...?
WE HAVE NO CHOICE.

MAKING MUMMIES

The Egyptians preserved their dead by a process called mummification. It was thought to allow people to live forever after death. The Egyptians believed that everyone had a *Ka* and a *Ba*. The *Ka* was the person's double, or soul, and the *Ba* was like the spirit. To live forever, the *Ka* and *Ba* needed to be reunited in the body after death. So it was important to stop the body from rotting. A decayed body meant an unhappy *Ka*—and misery in the afterlife.

THE *BA* BIRD

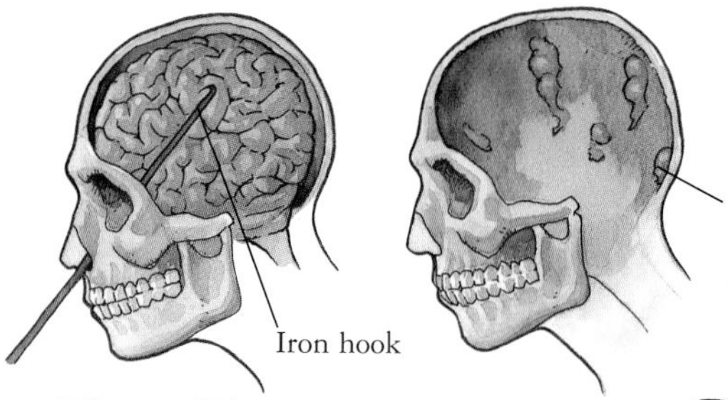

Iron hook

Broken-up brain ran out through the nose

NOSE TRICK

To remove the brain, a hook was pushed through a nostril and rotated vigorously for 20 minutes. This broke up the brain, turning it into a gluelike substance that could be drained out through the nose. The skull was then turned over and washed out with preservatives.

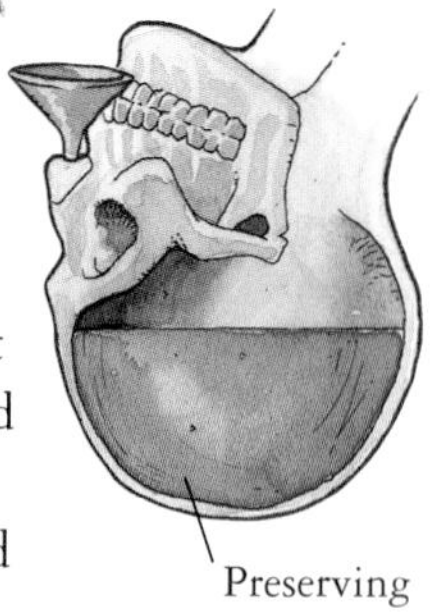

Preserving resin

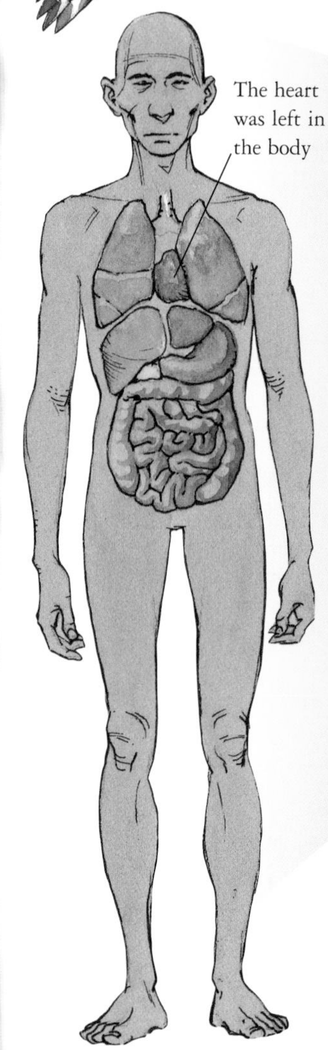

The heart was left in the body

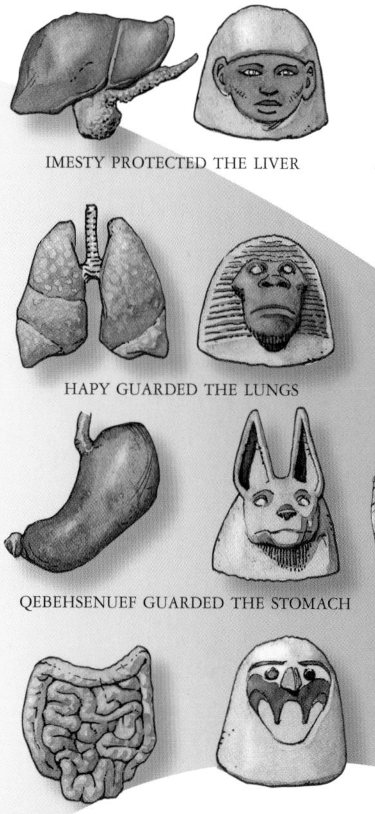

IMESTY PROTECTED THE LIVER

HAPY GUARDED THE LUNGS

QEBEHSENUEF GUARDED THE STOMACH

DUAMUTEF WATCHED OVER THE INTESTINES

PRESERVING THE ORGANS

When people were mummified, the lungs, stomach, intestines, and liver were removed. These organs were washed, dried, bandaged, and placed in special containers called canopic jars. The jars were sealed with lids in the form of each organ's guardian deity and placed beside the mummy inside the tomb.

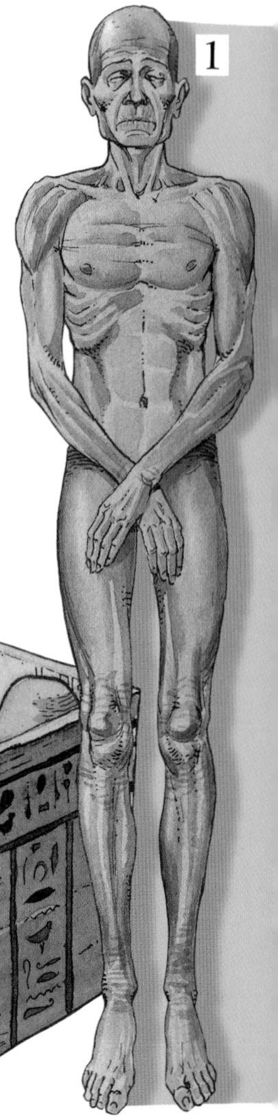

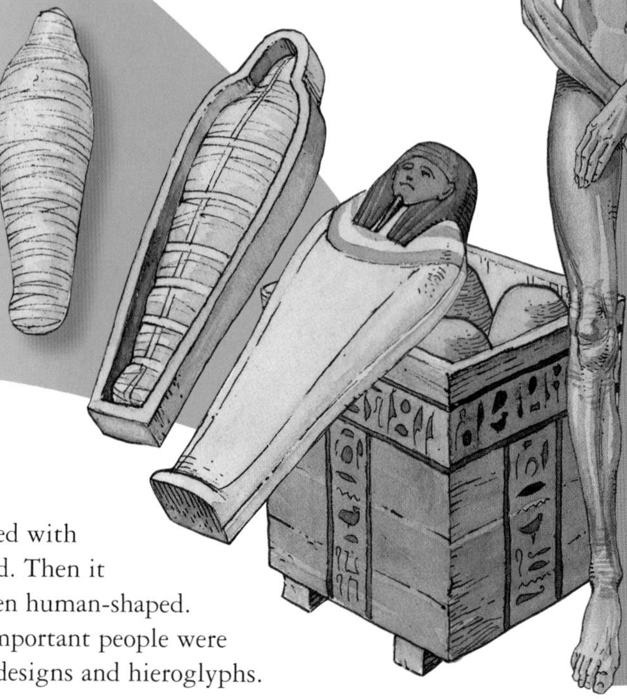

MUMMY CASES

The finished mummy was decorated with jewelry and makeup, and bandaged. Then it was placed in a wooden coffin, often human-shaped. Coffin cases of royalty and other important people were highly decorated with significant designs and hieroglyphs.

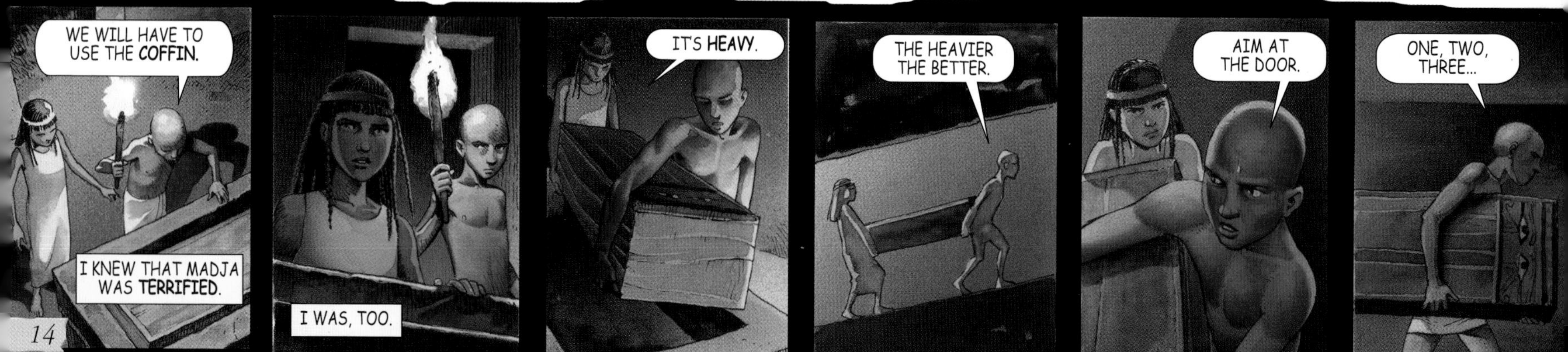

WE WILL HAVE TO USE THE COFFIN.
I KNEW THAT MADJA WAS TERRIFIED.
I WAS, TOO.
IT'S HEAVY.
THE HEAVIER THE BETTER.
AIM AT THE DOOR.
ONE, TWO, THREE...

Drying Out

The key to good mummy-making was getting the body as dry as possible. This was done by placing it on a special embalming table and smothering it with natron, a saltlike substance found in the desert.

The body remained covered for 40 days, during which time it lost about 75 percent of its weight.

Chief embalmer wears a jackal mask symbolizing Anubis, the god of the dead.

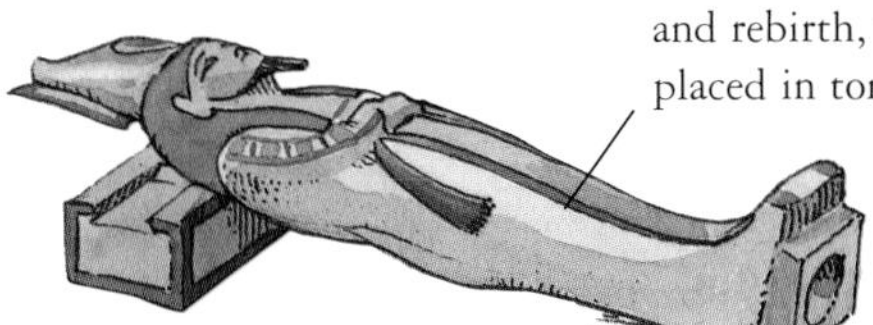

Models of Osiris, the god of death and rebirth, were placed in tombs.

Embalmer pours natron onto body

Chief embalmer leads magic chants

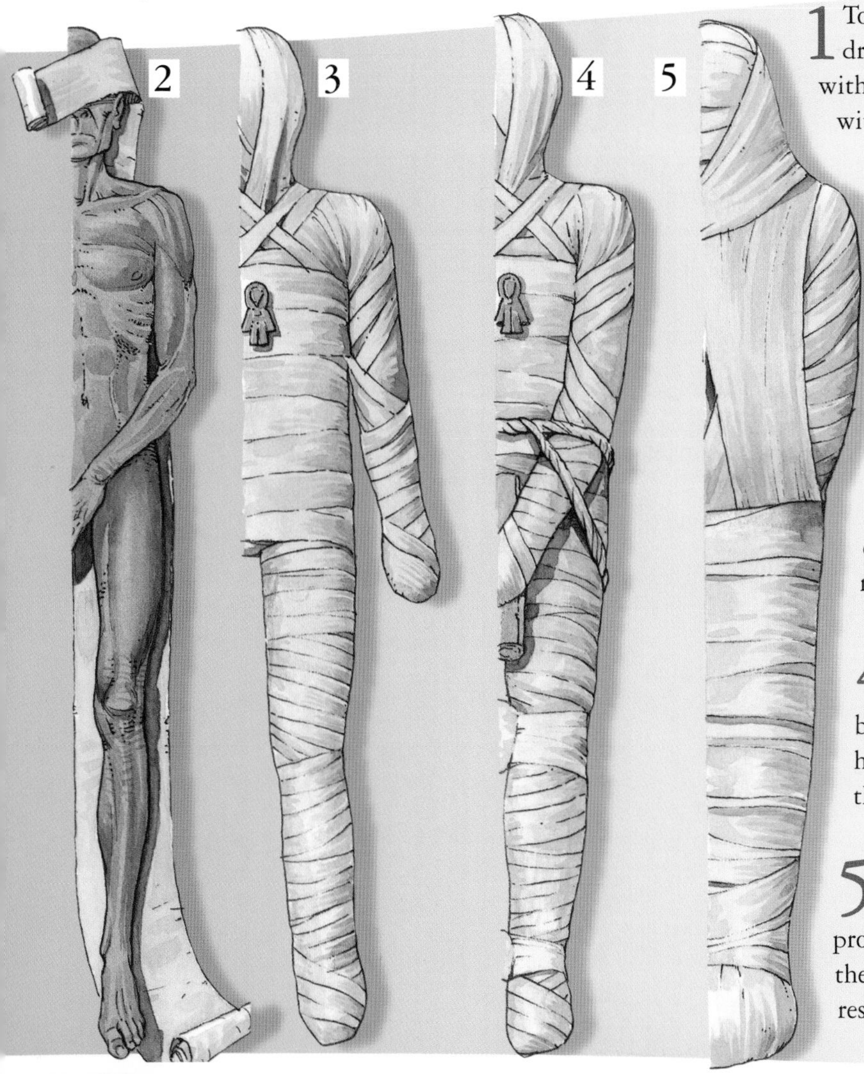

1 To restore its natural shape, the dried-out corpse was stuffed with fresh natron and rags scented with sweet-smelling oils.

2 Artificial eyes were inserted into the skull. The body was coated with resin and tightly bandaged to protect it.

3 Bandaging the body was a religious ritual that took 15 days. The linen bandages, often made from old clothes, were soaked in resin to stiffen them.

4 Protective amulets or charms were placed on the body in key places such as the heart and wrapped up with the bandages.

5 Securely tied with hundreds of yards of bandage, and protected with magic charms, the body was now a suitable residence for the eternal *Ka*.

MUMMY CASE

Story continues on next page

WHO KNOWS WHAT KENAMUN WOULD DO.
WE HAD TO FIND OUT WHERE KENAMUN HAD HIDDEN THE STOLEN TREASURE.
HE WILL SUSPECT HIS OWN MEN.
WE HAD EXPOSED KENAMUN'S SECRET ENTRANCE.
LET US GET AWAY FROM THIS PLACE.

THUD!
CRASH!
HELP!
LORD SOBEK PROTECT US!

STORY CONTINUED FROM PREVIOUS PAGE

HOUSE OF THE DEAD

Kenamun is the chief embalmer in the House of the Dead—a building or tented enclosure where bodies were mummified. They were sometimes built in the desert outside towns because of the smell and the flies. The mummification process was a religious ritual that lasted 70 days.

7 Drying out

Empty corpses were laid on wide, wooden or stone embalming tables and covered with natron. This technique was developed from earlier methods of drying in hot sand.

6 Clean On The Inside

After the organs had been removed, the body cavity was cleaned out and rinsed with palm wine. Meanwhile, the organs were stored in canopic jars.

5 Organ Donor

Watched by the Chief Embalmer, a jackal-headed priest of Anubis, the god of the dead, the body was washed. It was then cut open and the brains and internal organs were pulled out.

1 Grieving Relatives

When a dead body was carried to the House of the Dead, the entire family came out to wail and cry—sometimes with hired mourners to add professional tears.

2 Body In A Box

The body arrived in a plain wooden box.

3 Welcoming Priest

A priest welcomed the family at the door and showed them into the entrance foyer.

4 Entrance Foyer

Shielded from the sight (but not the smell) of the grisly operations going on inside, the family registered the body and selected a style of mummification and coffin.

STORY CONTINUES ON NEXT PAGE

8 Birds of Prey

Eagles swooped overhead, eager to snatch a tasty morsel of human flesh.

9 Taking a Break

While a corpse is carried from the drying room, the workers take a break in their covered rest area. Here they ate, drank, played board games—or just took a nap.

10 Bird Scarer

The priest employed young boys to scare away birds of prey and other desert scavengers, such as wild dogs and cats.

11 Spicing It Up

In this corner, the heart was packed with bags of spices and herbs, and padded out with linen and sawdust.

12 Bandages

When the first bandages went on, every finger and toe was wrapped individually. Sometimes body parts were mixed up, so the body of one person might be mummified with someone else's head!

13 Cover Up

Each mummy was wrapped with as many as 20 alternating layers of bandages—in total, up to 2,690 square feet (250 square meters), or half the size of a basketball court! At the same time, the linen was brushed with resin.

CONTINUED FROM PREVIOUS PAGE

NEXT MORNING, I ACCOMPANIED **FATHER** TO WORK.
I HAD TO **SPEAK** TO HIM.
FATHER IS A **PRIEST**...
...IN THE **TEMPLE OF SOBEK**.
THE VERY **GOD** WHOSE **CURSE** LAY **HEAVY ON MY** HEAD!

1 STONE NEEDLE

Stone obelisks outside the temple pointed to the sun and were carved with inscriptions in praise of the gods and the pharaoh.

2 ON GUARD

Crocodile-headed statues guarded the entrance to the temple. They wore headdresses of sun disks and feathers on their horny heads.

3 GATEWAY

A ceremonial gateway of tapering towers joined by a bridge, known as a pylon, rose above temple entrances. Only priests, the king and high-ranking officials could go beyond this point.

4 PHARAOH POWER

The temple walls were covered with scenes of the pharaoh's great victories—real or imaginary.

I KNEW IT WOULD NOT BE EASY TO TALK TO HIM.
YOU KNOW HOW **BUSY** THE TEMPLE IS...
AND FATHER IS ONE OF THE MOST **IMPORTANT** PRIESTS.
HIS DUTIES ARE MANY.
WHILE HE PREPARED THE **OFFERINGS**, I WAITED FOR MY MOMENT.
I FELT THE PRESENCE OF **SOBEK** ALL AROUND ME.
IT MADE ME **SHIVER**.

11 **Sacred Space**
Only priests and the pharaoh could approach the shrine of Sobek, lying at the dark, mysterious heart of the temple. Only the priests were thought to have the power to understand the god's wishes.

10 **Feeding the God**
Just like people, gods in ancient Egypt needed to eat. The priests prepared regular meals, which were laid before the image of the god in the morning and evening and cleared away later. The priests were permitted to eat the leftovers, once the god had had its fill!

9 **Priestly Sanctuary**
Only the important priests and the pharaoh were allowed to enter the temple's inner rooms. They performed religious rituals in these rooms.

8 **Vital Support**
Giant stone columns held up the roof. They were decorated with painted designs of papyrus plants with closed flowers.

7 **Sacred Pool**
Behind the temple, in a safely walled-off pool, real-life sacred crocodiles lazed in the sunshine. The priests sometimes used water from the sacred lake to perform rituals in the temple.

6 **Temple Courtyard**
Carved crocodile images adorned the walls of the temple courtyard, which was open to the sky. Sobek was shown as either all-crocodile or half-man, half-crocodile.

5 **Royal High-Priest**
The pharaoh was the high priest of all temples. Scenes on the courtyard walls showed him making offerings to Sobek, reminding people that their king was a vital link between them and the gods.

Temple City

The largest temples were rebuilt and enlarged over many centuries, until they covered several acres. They were important centers of commerce, as well as religion. The largest temples employed dozens of people, owned farming land and mines, and even engaged in foreign trade. The walled temple itself—a maze of rooms, pylons, courtyards, shrines and statues—was surrounded by storehouses, workshops, workers' homes and priest schools.

Temple of Sobek

All over Egypt, people praised Sobek, the crocodile god—but the Fayum region, where Methen lives, was the god's main place of worship. Priests in the town of Crocodilopolis, for example, were so croc-obsessed they adorned live specimens with gold, and fed them honey cakes and meat! This most ferocious of gods was also honored in spectacular temples, where priests guarded, cared for, and worshipped the god's image day and night.

Story continues on next page

HAVE MERCY ON US, SOBEK.

THE RITUALS SEEMED TO TAKE FOREVER.
THE GOD MUST BE WASHED AND DRESSED.
ANOINTED WITH PERFUMES
ADORNED WITH JEWELS.
SERVED THE OFFERINGS....
I COULDN'T WAIT ANY LONGER. I ASKED FATHER...
...ABOUT THE FATE OF THE PYRAMID THIEVES.
HIS ONLY ANSWER...
SOBEK WILL BE AVENGED.
BUT MADJA AND I HAD COMMITTED SACRILEGE, TOO.

NILOMETER

The River of Life

The civilization of ancient Egypt depended on the mighty Nile River. Every year, between June and September, monsoon rains fell thousands of miles to the south and caused the river to rise and flood the surrounding countryside. The flood, called the "Inundation," brought fresh life to the dry fields along its banks. In order to measure the height of the river and thus predict when the flood would arrive, the Egyptians used measuring devices called "nilometers." The readings from nilometers were carefully recorded.

Farmers returned to their fields when the flood waters went down in the fall.

Nilometers

Ruled horizontal lines were cut into steps along the Nile's banks to measure the all-important level of the river. Many temples had their own nilometers, which were thought to gauge the gods' favor as well as the Nile's height.

Flood Waters

As the Nile's water level rose during the rainy season in Central Africa, land on either side was submerged: the higher the flood, the more land would be underwater—making it fertile for planting crops. When the floods reached a mid-level, the Egyptians believed that Hapy, the god of the Nile, had smiled on them.

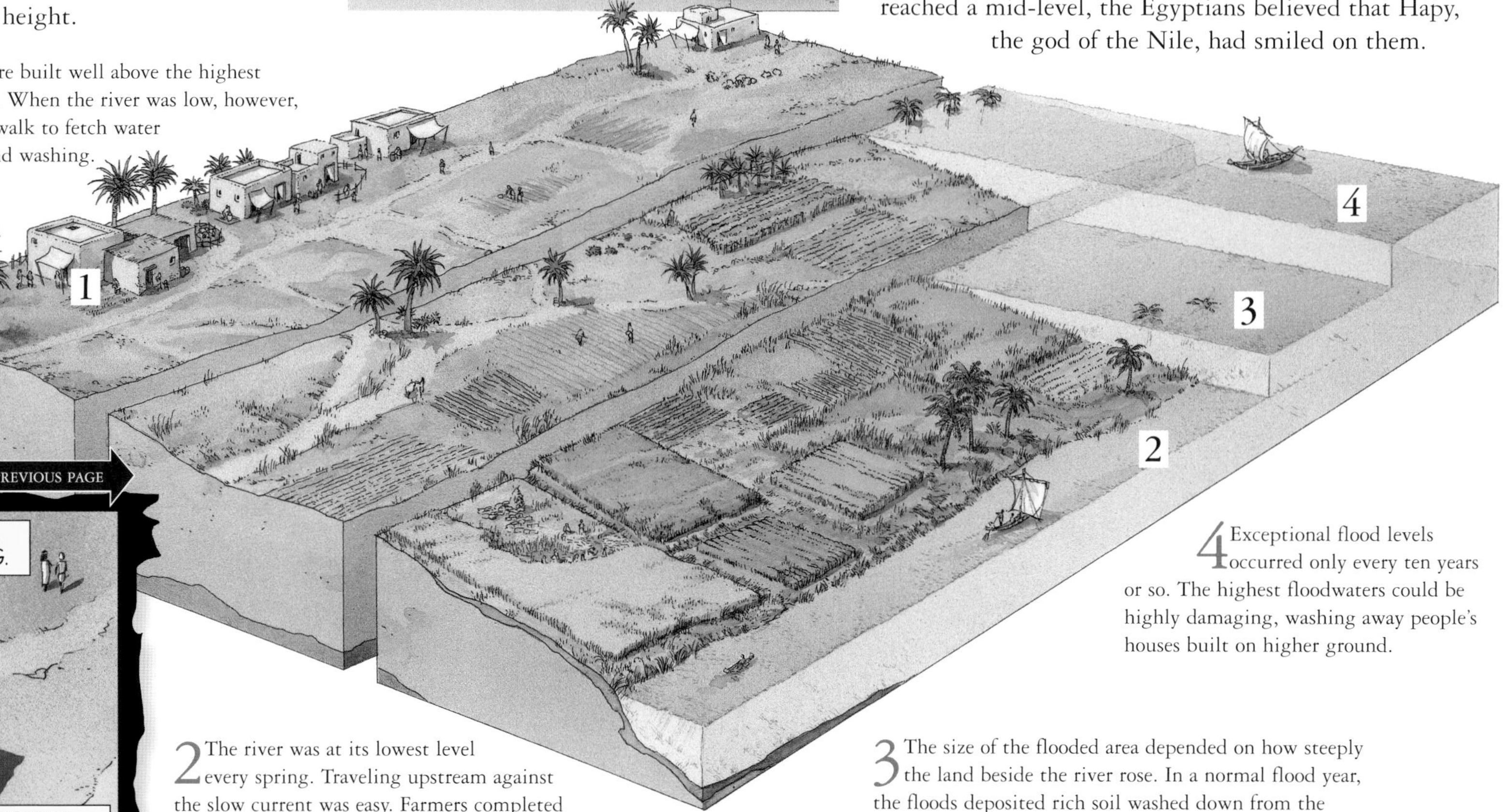

1 Houses were built well above the highest flood level. When the river was low, however, it was a long walk to fetch water for cooking and washing.

2 The river was at its lowest level every spring. Traveling upstream against the slow current was easy. Farmers completed the harvest before the river rose again.

3 The size of the flooded area depended on how steeply the land beside the river rose. In a normal flood year, the floods deposited rich soil washed down from the highlands. This was dug and planted in the late fall.

4 Exceptional flood levels occurred only every ten years or so. The highest floodwaters could be highly damaging, washing away people's houses built on higher ground.

Continued from previous page

I MET MADJA THAT EVENING.
WE DECIDED TO SEARCH KENAMUN'S BOAT.

THERE IT IS.
LISTEN... SOMEONE'S DOWN THERE.
TWO GUARDS WERE TALKING.
...THEY'VE FOUND TWO OF KENAMUN'S MEN...
NAKHT AND IAHAMES, WITH THE LIMP...
"THEY WERE FOUND IN THE DESERT..."
"NO MARKS ON THEIR BODIES."
LORD INI SUSPECTS POISON.
I WONDER WHO THEY GOT ON THE WRONG SIDE OF?

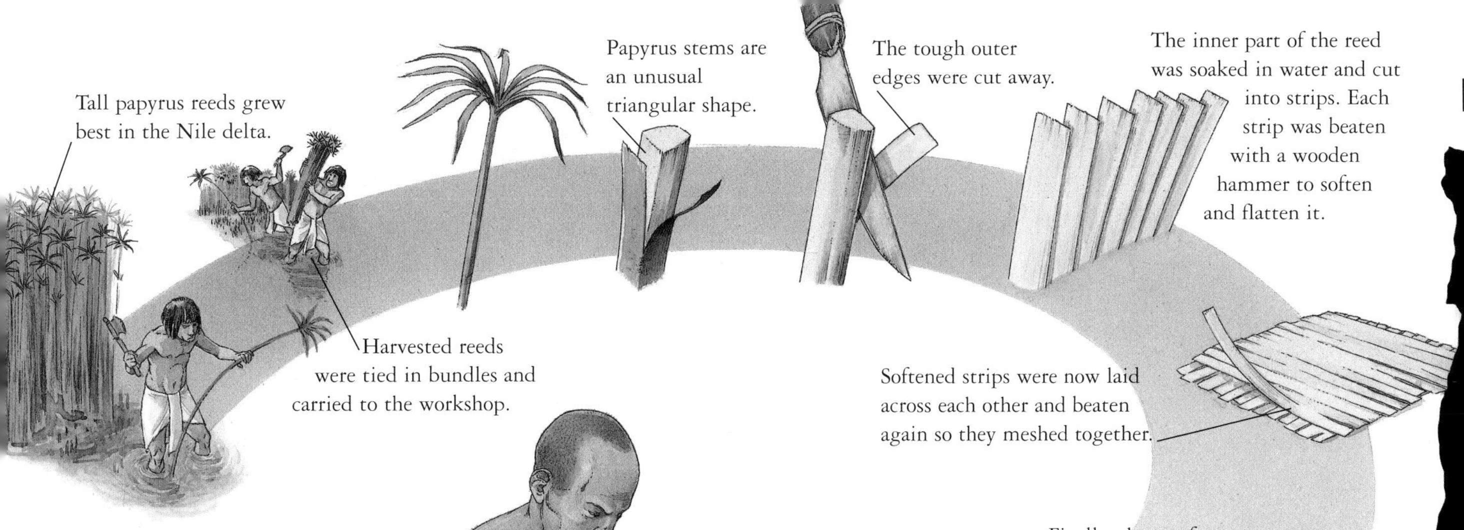

Tall papyrus reeds grew best in the Nile delta.
Harvested reeds were tied in bundles and carried to the workshop.
Papyrus stems are an unusual triangular shape.
The tough outer edges were cut away.
The inner part of the reed was soaked in water and cut into strips. Each strip was beaten with a wooden hammer to soften and flatten it.
Softened strips were now laid across each other and beaten again so they meshed together.

Papyrus

The papyrus reeds that grew beside the Nile were made into boats, baskets, ropes, and a type of paper. Papyrus paper (just called "papyrus") was first made over 5,000 years ago and was used for almost 3,500 years. The sheets were not bound into books, but were joined together in long rolls. Normally, just the inside was written on, and the outside was left blank.

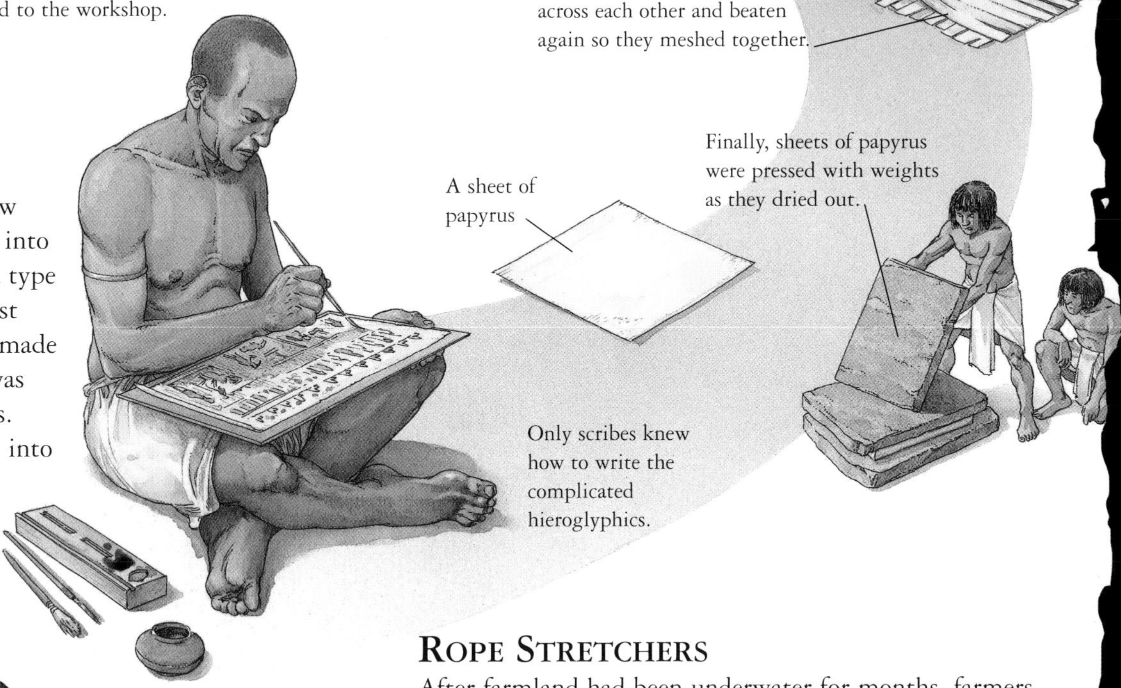

A sheet of papyrus
Finally, sheets of papyrus were pressed with weights as they dried out.
Only scribes knew how to write the complicated hieroglyphics.

Rope Stretchers

After farmland had been underwater for months, farmers often had little idea where their fields had been. To solve this problem, surveyors, scribes, supervisors, and inspectors would arrive with ropes to measure the land at low water. They kept a record of the measurements, and then, after the floods had gone down, the "rope stretchers" returned and measured out the fields again. These officials also fixed the amount of tax the farmers had to pay.

Story continues on next page

KENAMUN KNOWS MUCH ABOUT POISONS!
LOOK, THE GUARDS ARE LEAVING.
KENAMUN SHOULD BE HERE BY NOW.
LET'S GO AND LOOK FOR HIM.
RISKING ALL, WE MADE OUR WAY TO THE BOAT.
HURRY!
I KNEW WE HAD TO BE QUICK...

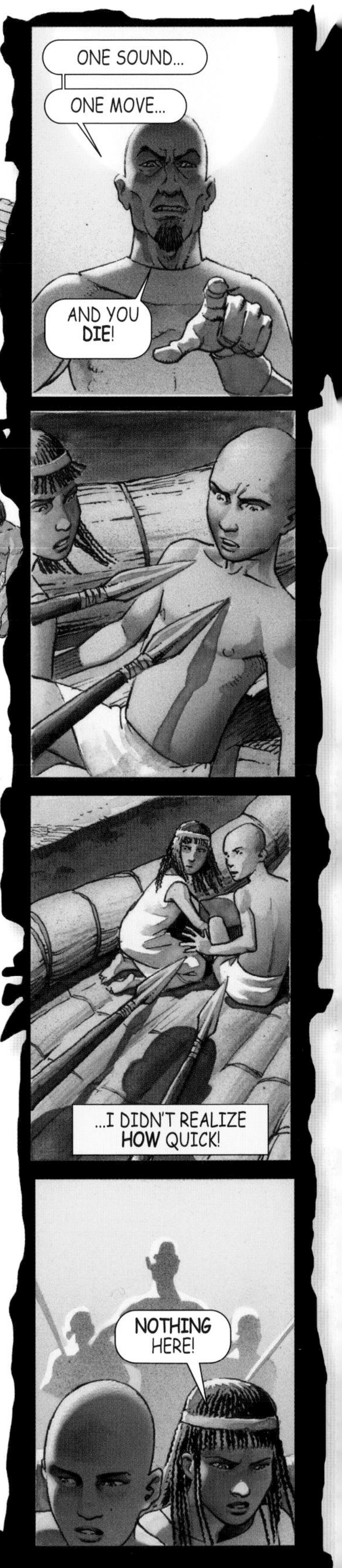

NOTHING HERE!
...I DIDN'T REALIZE HOW QUICK!
ONE SOUND...
ONE MOVE...
AND YOU DIE!

CONTINUED FROM PREVIOUS PAGE

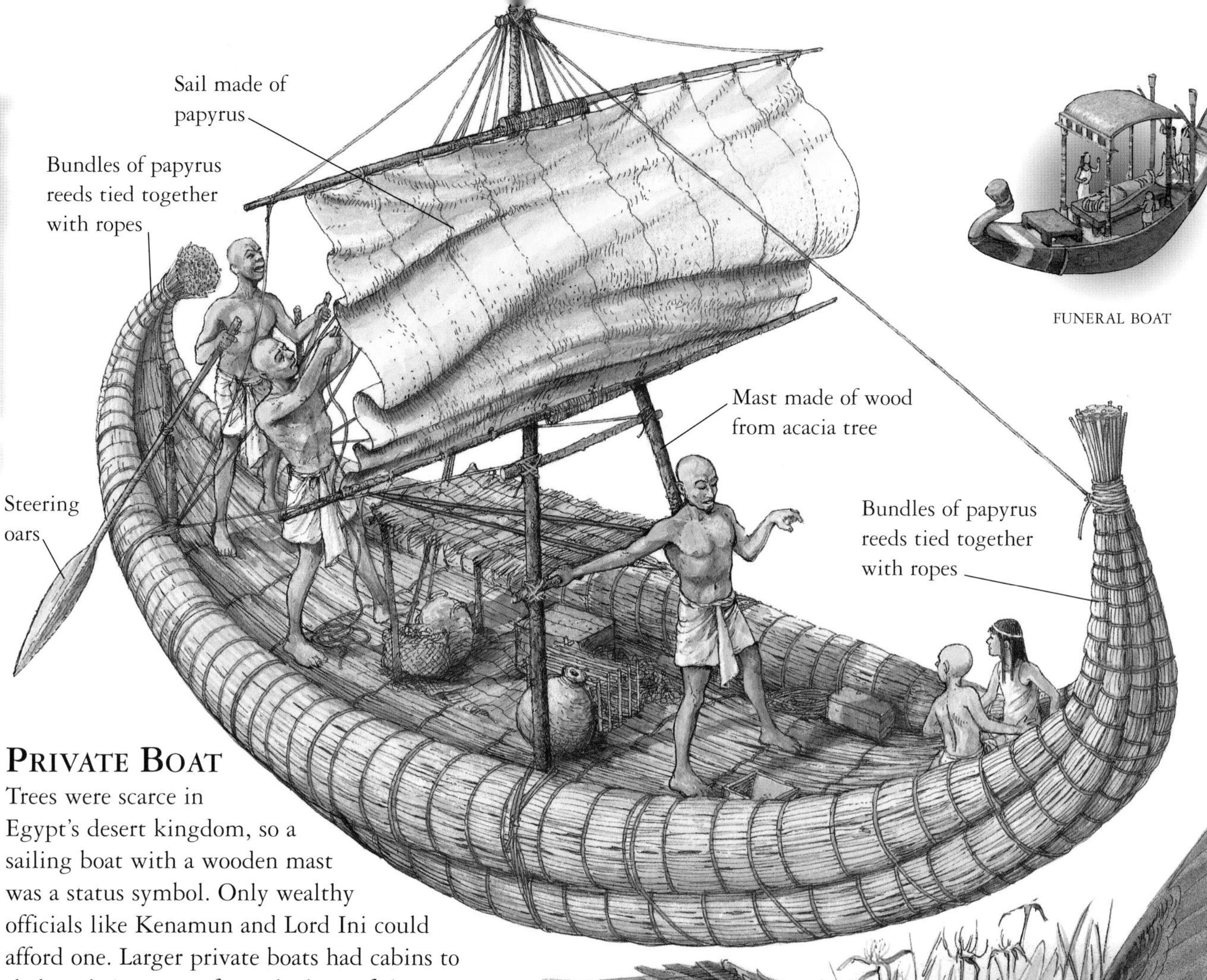

FUNERAL BOAT

PRIVATE BOAT

Trees were scarce in Egypt's desert kingdom, so a sailing boat with a wooden mast was a status symbol. Only wealthy officials like Kenamun and Lord Ini could afford one. Larger private boats had cabins to shelter their owners from the heat of the sun.

ON THE NILE

The Nile River was Egypt's "freeway." People went everywhere by water, in many different types of boats. The smallest craft were simple fishing canoes made of papyrus reeds. The largest vessels were merchant ships carrying goods to and from Egypt and container barges carrying statues and large stones for building. River travel was so vital that the symbol (hieroglyph) for "going north" was a ship with sails down, while "going south" was a ship with sails up.

MY BLOOD WAS AS ICE.
SO THIS WAS LORD SOBEK'S REVENGE FOR THOSE WHO DISOBEYED HIM!
FORGIVE ME, METHEN. PLEASE! I BROUGHT THIS UPON YOU.
DON'T SPEAK LIKE THAT, MADJA...
SILENCE!
WE DRAW CLOSE TO THE PLACE.
PREPARE THE VAGABONDS FOR THEIR SWIM!

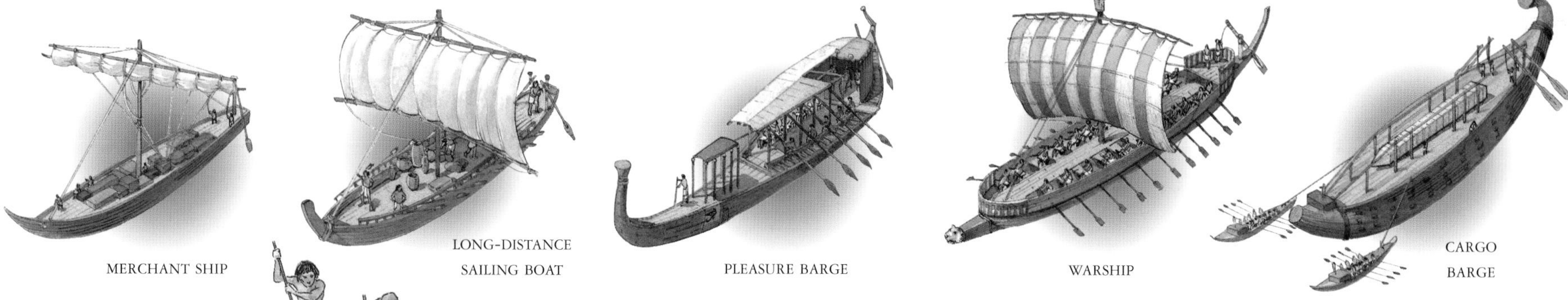

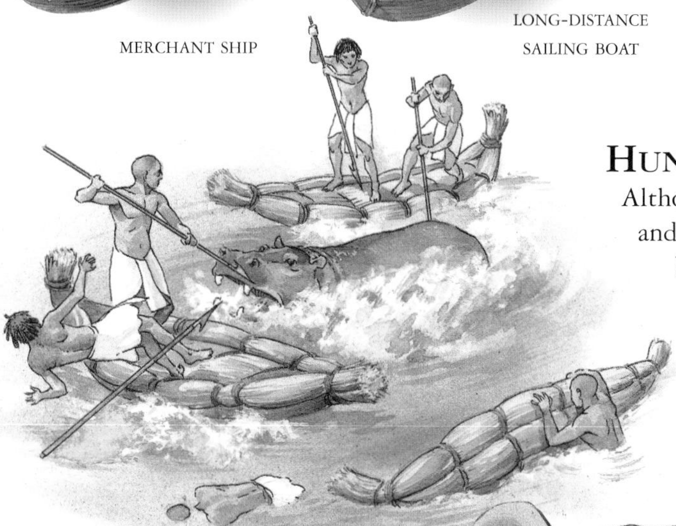

Hunting in the Nile

Although most food was provided by farming, Egyptians also fished and hunted in the Nile. Fishermen took to the waters in simple boats made of reeds to catch fish with hooks or nets. Teams of men in boats hunted hippos with spears (*left*)—these wild animals could be a danger to people in boats and to their crops on land. Egyptians also hunted wild birds, such as herons and ducks, with special throwsticks (*below*).

Story continues on next page

HELP!
AHHHHH!

HA! HA! HA!
THE SERVANTS FORCED US TO STAND. JUST THEN...
LOOK OUT, MASTER!
HIPPOS!

The Great House

The word "pharaoh" originally meant "great house," the place where the king lived. Later, it came to mean the ruling king himself or herself. The pharaoh was chief priest and judge, army commander and ruler all rolled into one. Meeting the pharaoh at court must have been a genuinely nerve-wracking experience!

BIG-GAME HUNTING

Kings liked to be thought of as great hunters. To help their heroics, animals were rounded up and held in game parks. Here the royal hunters could be sure of making a spectacular—and simple—kill. Their victims included wild bulls, lions, and even ostriches.

VULTURE AND COBRA HEADBAND

RED CROWN

WHITE CROWN

DOUBLE CROWN

BLUE CROWN

Crowns of Egypt

In ancient Egypt, crowns were probably made of colored cloth, leather, or metal. Pharaohs had many styles of crowns to choose from. The earliest was the White Crown of Upper Egypt. When a single king ruled the whole land, this was combined with the Red Crown of Lower Egypt to make the Double Crown. Alternatively, they could wear a blue crown adorned with golden disks or a striped headband called a circlet.

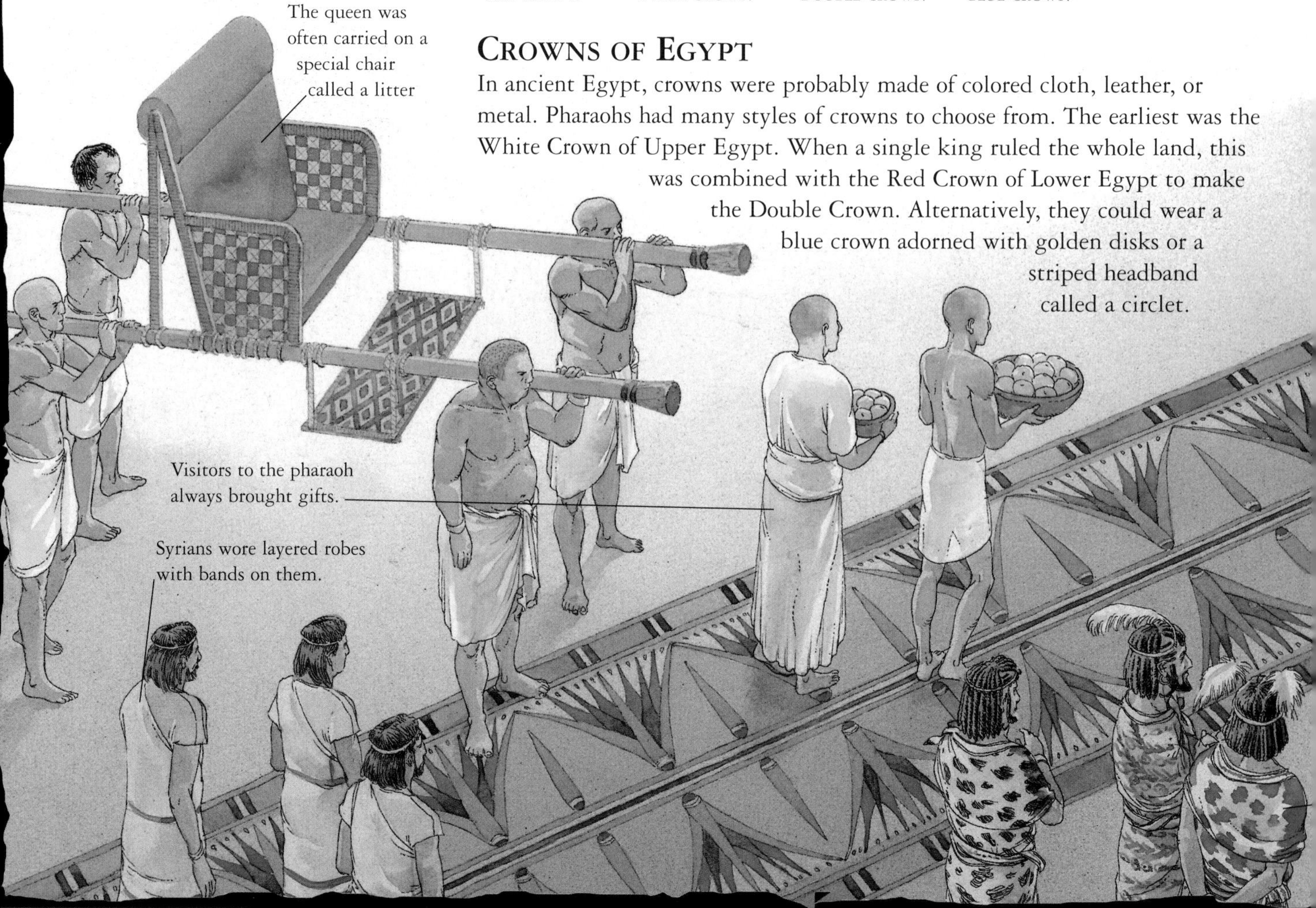

Continued from previous page

FIND THEM, IDIOTS!
LOOK OUT!

HURRY!
WE'RE NOT SAFE YET—LOOK!
QUICK—IN HERE!
WE HID IN THE PAPYRUS REEDS ALL NIGHT.
WE WOKE AT DAWN AND CHECKED THAT WE WERE SAFE.
WHAT SHALL WE DO NOW?

The pharaoh was always accompanied by his private guards, as well as by courtiers and musicians.

In public, the pharaoh held a crook and flail—the symbols of royal power.

Scribes kept written records of important events.

People from the lands bordering Egypt came to pay their respects to the Pharaoh to ensure peace between their countries.

Courtiers waved fans made of dyed ostrich feathers to keep the pharaoh cool.

The floor in the throne room was tiled and painted with murals depicting beautiful gardens.

People from Libya typically dressed in clothes made of brightly colored animal hides with feathers in their hair.

Morning Ritual

The pharaoh was expected to win the favor of his fellow gods so that Egypt would prosper. He performed a ritual every morning, burning incense to the sun god Amon-Ra.

Throne Room

The most splendid place in the pharaoh's palace was the throne room. Here, the pharaoh held royal audiences, when officials and nobles came to him to read reports about the country or make requests. On these occasions, the pharaoh sat on a covered platform, like an altar or a stage. Since the pharaoh was a son of the gods, the throne room was a holy place.

WE MUST TELL LORD INI..
HE WILL SAVE US.
WE RETURNED TO THE TOWN...
AND HEADED FOR THE PALACE OF LORD INI.
I EXPLAINED WHO MY FATHER WAS...
AND WE WERE GRANTED AN AUDIENCE...
WITH HIS LORDSHIP.

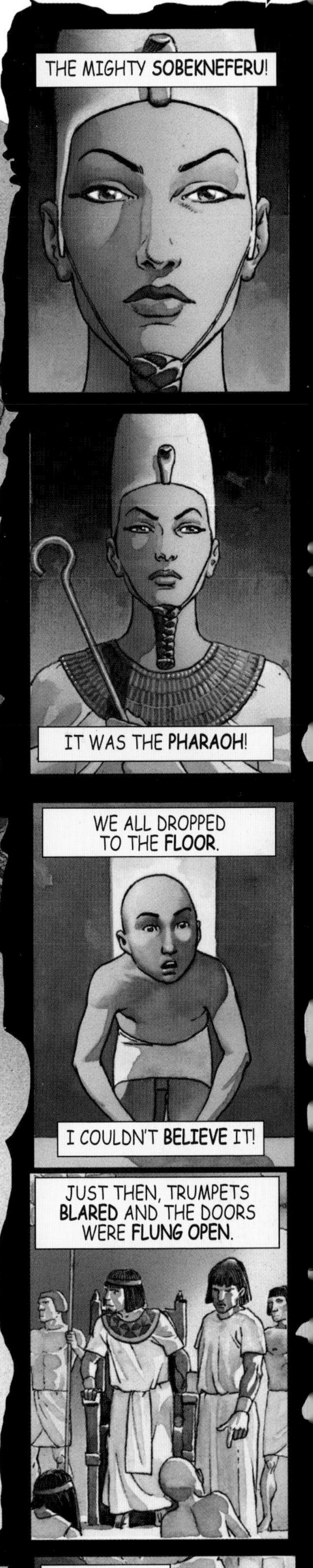

JUST THEN, TRUMPETS BLARED AND THE DOORS WERE FLUNG OPEN.
I COULDN'T BELIEVE IT!
WE ALL DROPPED TO THE FLOOR.
IT WAS THE PHARAOH!
THE MIGHTY SOBEKNEFERU!

STORY CONTINUES ON NEXT PAGE

CONTINUED FROM PREVIOUS PAGE

KEEPING THE PEACE

In general, the Egyptians seem to have been a law-abiding, practical people who based their law on common sense. Many laws were only clearly written down in the Late Period (747-332 BCE). Throughout the early ancient Egyptian period, high officials often acted as judges, although in later times specialist judges were appointed and wore gold pendants. The king, of course, was the supreme judge in any dispute.

THE PHARAOH GLOWERED AT US.
WHY ARE THESE CHILDREN HERE, LORD INI?
LORD INI EXPLAINED OUR BUSINESS.
I DO NOT LIKE WHAT I HEAR.

GODDESS OF JUSTICE

The goddess *Maat* represented justice. She was worshiped throughout Egypt—even by other gods!

Curved sword called a *khepesh*
The Medjay thickened their hair with wax to form a kind of protective helmet!

The word "Medjay" became the ancient Egyptian term for "policeman."

SETTLING QUARRELS

Town councils of senior citizens normally settled day-to-day squabbles. The council, known as the *kenbet*, heard both sides of the case before making a decision. Scribes kept a record of the proceedings. It was also possible to ask a god or goddess, via a priest acting as an oracle, to decide a case. The priest would then let the accused know the god's answer!

POLICE FORCE

The Egyptians had two types of police—guards and enforcers. Groups of guards patrolled the desert to fend off raiders. The task of guarding frontiers, mines, and other important sites was largely in the hands of the Medjay—a fierce tribal people from Nubia, the land south of Egypt. The job of enforcing the law, arresting wrongdoers, and punishing the guilty was carried out by men known as *sa-per*.

GO, BRING KENAMUN HITHER!
AFRAID TO MOVE,
WE WAITED.
WHEN KENAMUN ARRIVED, HE DENIED EVERYTHING.
IT IS A SHAMEFUL FALSEHOOD, YOUR MAJESTY!
WHERE IS THE EVIDENCE?
I SWEAR BY SOBEK THAT WE ARE HONEST.

PAINTED FRIEZE SHOWING THE TRIAL AND PUNISHMENT OF CORRUPT TAX INSPECTORS

Punishment

Punishments were intended to be short, sharp shocks. The most common form of punishment was a public beating, with the criminal kneeling and tied to a short pole. The number of strokes depended on the crime. Punishments for more serious crimes included mutilation (cutting off the nose, for example), wounding, or death. Less violent punishments included fines, confiscation of property, and exile (being sent to live outside Egypt). The Egyptians considered all foreigners to be completely uncivilized, so exile was a particularly shameful punishment.

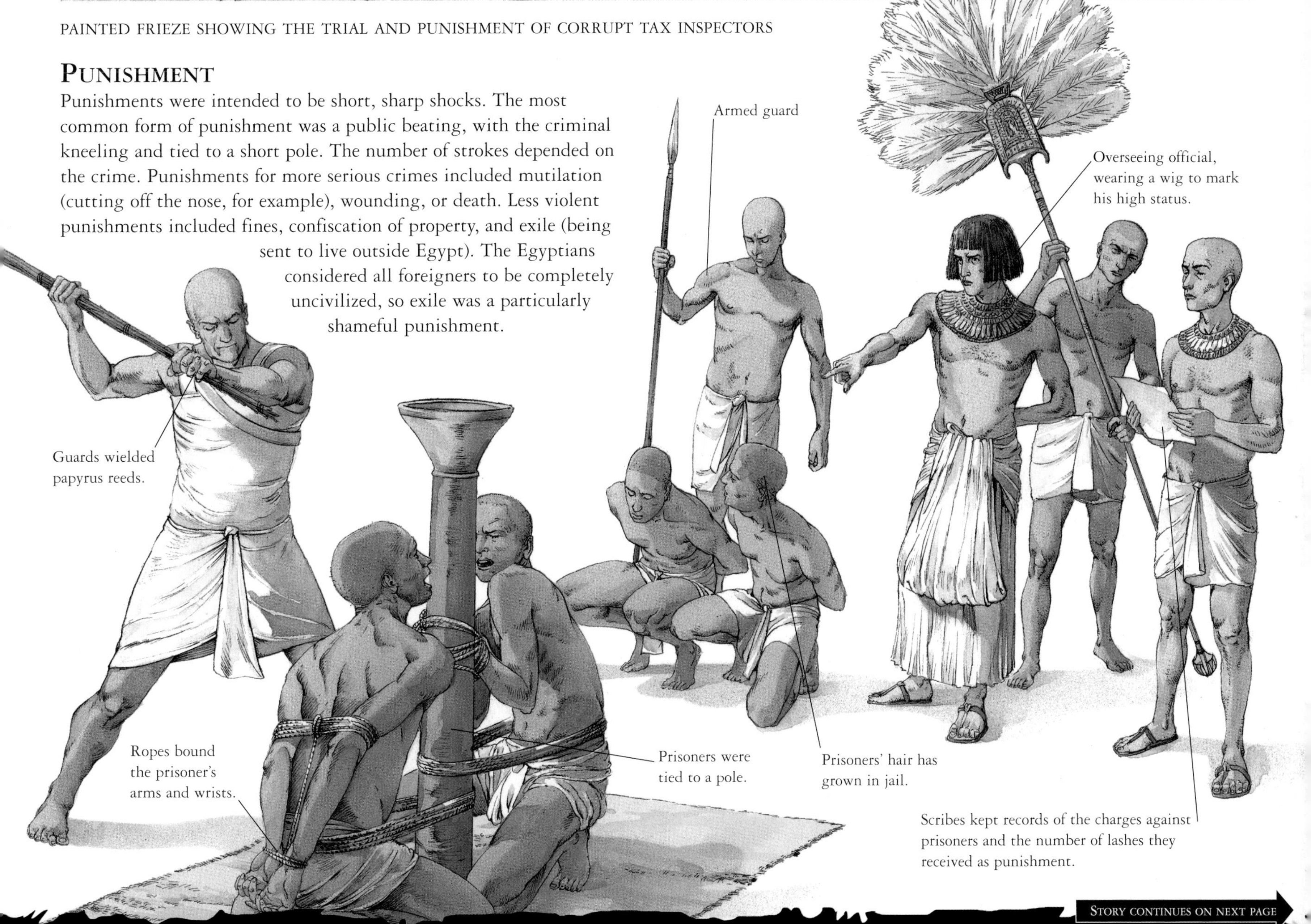

Armed guard
Overseeing official, wearing a wig to mark his high status.
Guards wielded papyrus reeds.
Ropes bound the prisoner's arms and wrists.
Prisoners were tied to a pole.
Prisoners' hair has grown in jail.
Scribes kept records of the charges against prisoners and the number of lashes they received as punishment.

Story continues on next page

WHY WAS IAHAMES KILLED, SIRE?
DID HE KNOW TOO MUCH?
IGNORANT SLAVE! SLAY HER!
HARSH WORDS, KENAMUN.
YOUR BETROTHED, IS SHE NOT?
I BEG YOUR MAJESTY...
ORDER A SEARCH OF THE HOUSE OF THE DEAD.
SO BE IT.
WE WILL SEARCH THE HOUSE OF THE DEAD.
BUT, CHILDREN, IF NOTHING BE FOUND—YOU DIE!

CRAFTWORKING

Art and craft was a serious matter in ancient Egypt. At the back of an Egyptian's mind was a nagging worry that the universe and all its gods and people might one day pass away. They believed that if artists and craftworkers created perfect examples of things, this was less likely to happen. Unsurprisingly, top painters, sculptors, and craftworkers could become rich and respected citizens.

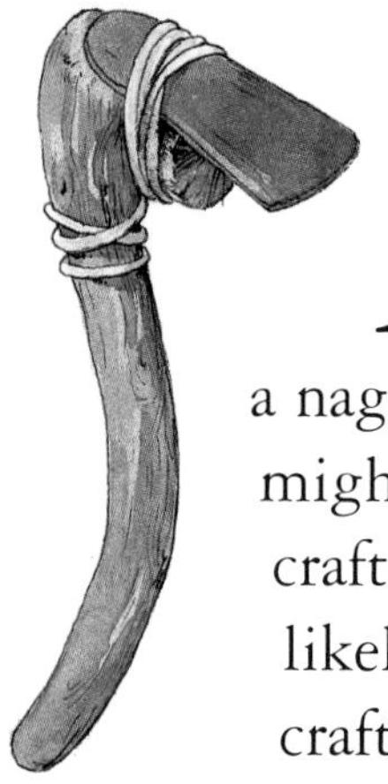

ADZE FOR SMOOTHING SURFACES

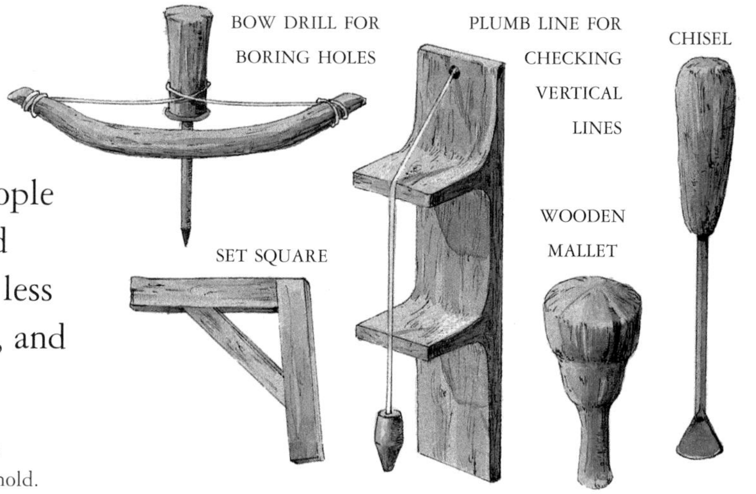

SILVER WORKERS

Craftworkers used copper and bronze to make tools, weapons, and jewelry. Silver was rare and more precious than gold—the gods' bones were said to be made of silver! Metalworking was a hard job, involving the carrying of many heavy loads. Metal foundries were dirty, smelly, and often dangerously hot, due to the open fires beneath the furnaces. Safety precautions were almost nonexistent.

WONDER WEAVE

Egyptian linen cloth was famous throughout the ancient world. The thread was made from the flax plant, then woven into cloth on broad looms. Extra-special cloth had gold thread woven with the linen.

SKILLED ARTISTS

Since the making of images was so important to ancient Egyptian society, artists and specialist craftworkers were important people. They enjoyed a much higher standard of living than farmers or ordinary craftworkers such as potters. However, much of the basic work was done by lowly helpers, leaving those in charge to add the finishing touches—and get all the praise.

CONTINUED FROM PREVIOUS PAGE

WE WERE ESCORTED TO THE HOUSE OF THE DEAD.
KENAMUN WAS MUTTERING AND CURSING.
SCANDALOUS...!
A MERE SLAVE!
THE SOLDIERS BEGAN TO SEARCH THE PLACE.
THEY OPENED POTS...
SEARCHED THE NATRON STORES...
AND UNRAVELED BANDAGES.
THEY WERE THOROUGH, LOOKING ALMOST EVERYWHERE.
WE HAVE FOUND NOTHING, SIR.

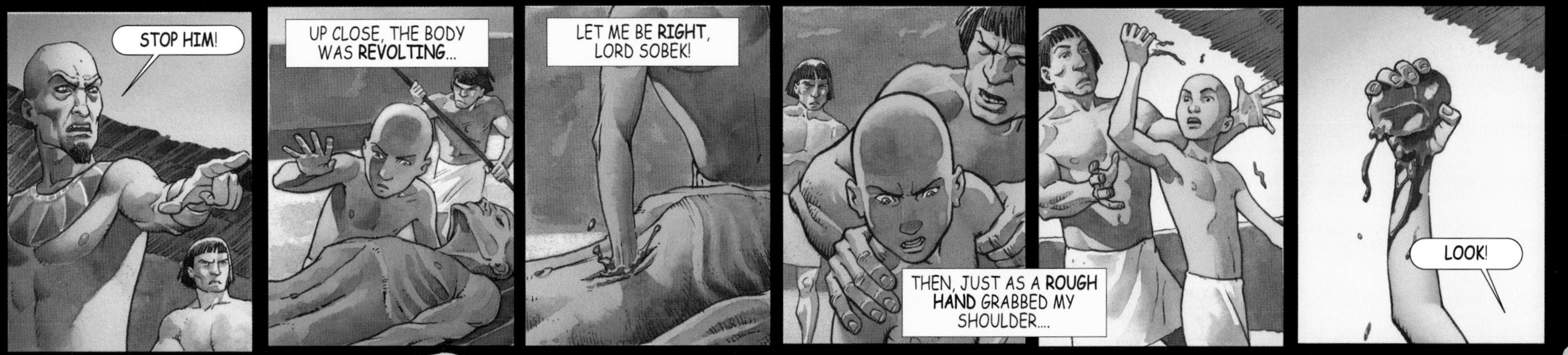

STORY CONTINUES ON NEXT PAGE

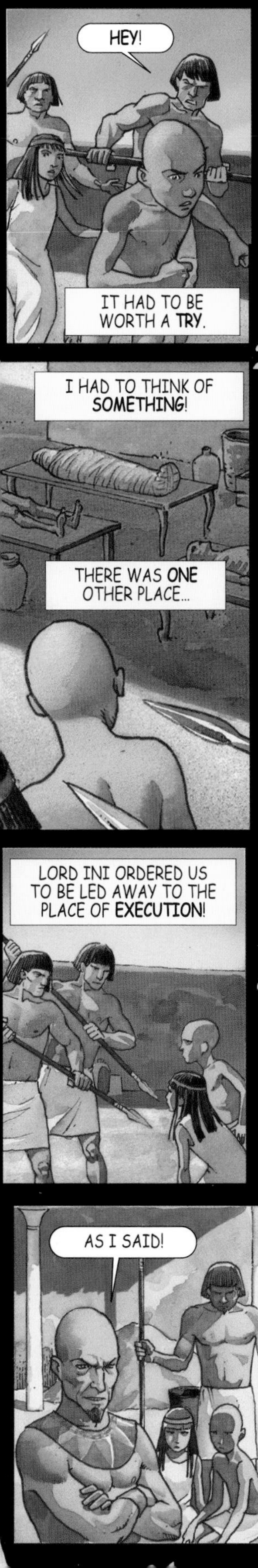

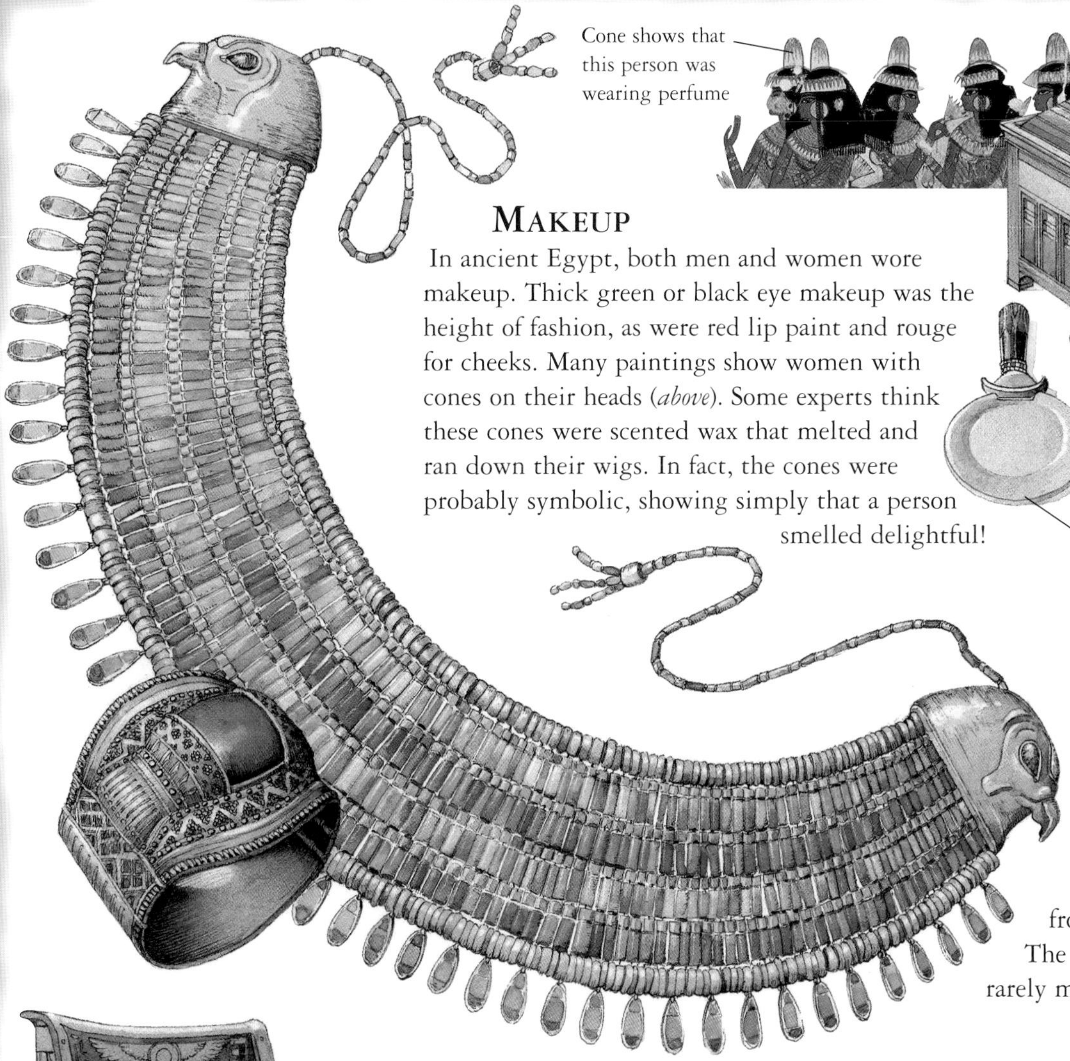

Makeup

In ancient Egypt, both men and women wore makeup. Thick green or black eye makeup was the height of fashion, as were red lip paint and rouge for cheeks. Many paintings show women with cones on their heads (*above*). Some experts think these cones were scented wax that melted and ran down their wigs. In fact, the cones were probably symbolic, showing simply that a person smelled delightful!

Worth Copying

When 19th-century Westerners first returned with Egyptian artifacts and furniture, the ancient style became the height of fashion from London to Moscow. The workmanship, however, rarely matched that of the originals.

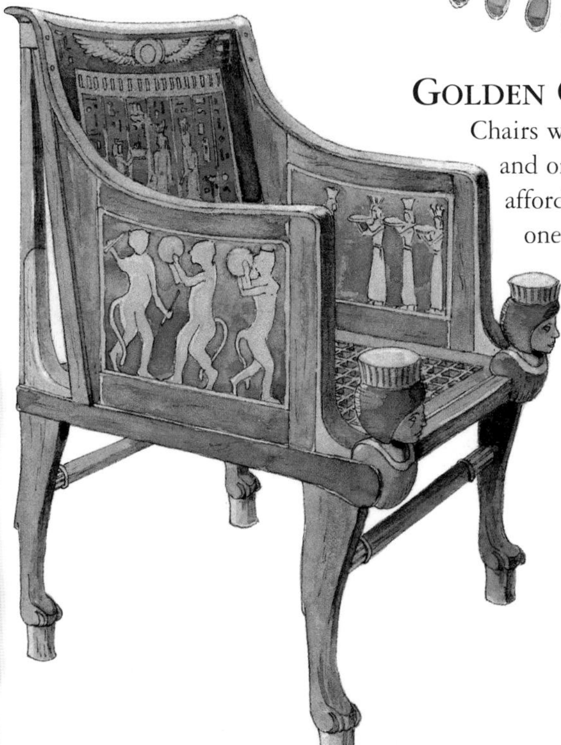

Golden Chair

Chairs were symbols of authority and only important people could afford beautiful seats like this one. Made for Tutankhamun's aunt, Sitamun, its wooden frame is overlaid with gold and silver.

Board Games

The Egyptians enjoyed board games, including Dogs and Jackals, played with pointed sticks carved with dog or jackal heads. The game of Senet was also immensely popular: everyone played it, from kings to servants.

CONTINUED FROM PREVIOUS PAGE

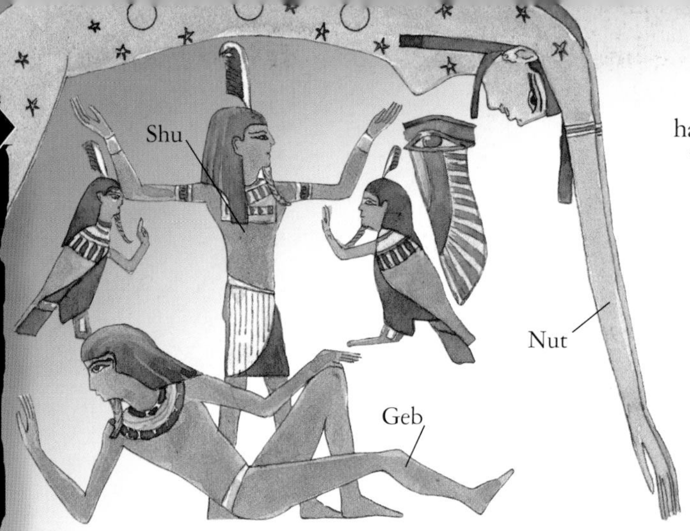

EYE SPY

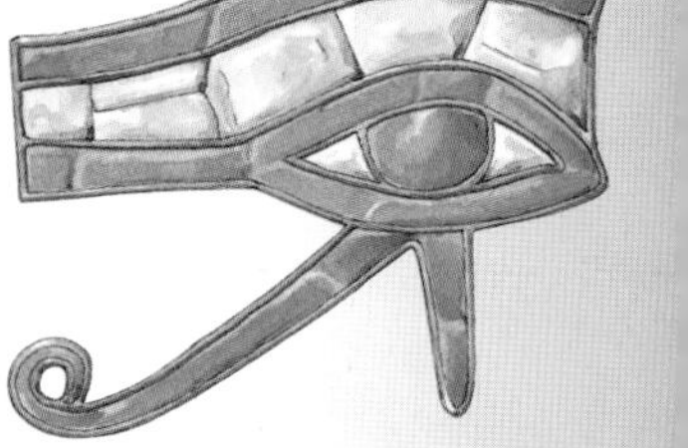

Horus, the pharaohs' own god, once had his missing left eye kindly restored by the goddess of love. After that, the Horus-eye (or *wedjat*-eye) became a very popular symbol of healing and protection. Horus-eye jewelry was often buried with the dead.

IN THE BEGINNING...

According to the Egyptians, the world began with the creator-god Atum ("the All") rising up from the waters of chaos. Two of his children, the air-god Shu and his sister-wife Tefnut (goddess of damp air) gave birth to Geb, the god of the Earth, and Nut, the overarching goddess of the sky.

HOLY HOMES

Certain deities were particularly useful around the house. The friendly she-hippo goddess, Tawaret (*left*), who sometimes had lion and/or crocodile limbs, kept an eye on women in childbirth. The dwarf Bes (*right*) was fierce but kept away evil spirits and helped couples to produce children. People often wore a carving of him around their necks for luck.

FACING THE GODS

The Egyptians worshiped hundreds of gods and goddesses, who were responsible for everything that happened, from the flooding of the Nile to the appearance of the sun in the sky. The Egyptians also believed that the gods judged them after death in the Underworld, a grim region where monsters lurked in dark corners. Only those who had lived good lives escaped.

3 HEART OF THE MATTER

In the Hall of Judgment, the heart of the deceased was placed on one side of a balance. To the ancient Egyptians, the heart was the center of a person's personality, containing all their memories. This is the reason the Egyptians took special care to leave the heart in the body of the deceased.

2 THOTH

Holding a reed pen, the ibis-headed god, Thoth, recorded the verdict on the deceased person's soul. Thoth was the god of writing and knowledge. He was associated with the moon, too, because his curved ibis beak looked like a crescent moon.

1 YOU ARE CHARGED...

Deep in the Underworld, a dead person (or, rather, his spirit, or soul) met the King of Death face to face. Quivering with fear, he listened to a list of the bad things he had done in his lifetime. He must then deny the charges. If successful, he moved on to the even more frightening "weighing of the heart" ceremony....

Devourer of the Dead

HE KNOCKED OVER A TABLE OF NATRON POTS...
AND HUMAN BODIES!
A CLOUD OF NATRON STUNG OUR EYES...
SEIZE HIM!
WHILE KENAMUN SPRINTED OUT OF THE HOUSE OF THE DEAD.
HE RAN AT GREAT SPEED TOWARD THE RIVER....
WHERE HE STOLE A SMALL BOAT!
HEY!

4 Perfect Balance

Anubis weighed the heart of the deceased—the essence of their being—against the Feather of *Maat*, which represented goodness and truth. If the two balanced exactly, the dead person was said to have spoken truly. He could then approach the throne of Osiris. The failures wished they had never existed….

5 The Incorruptible Judge

Osiris, the god of death and rebirth, presides over the judgment of a spirit, with his sister-wife Isis standing beside him. In legend, Osiris was once a living pharaoh who was murdered by his evil brother, Seth. However, the devotion of Isis allowed Osiris to defeat death and become a god.

6 Dead Watcher

The god Anubis—jackal-headed and the color of a rotting corpse—played a part in everything that happened after death. He kept an eye on mummification and offered a helping hand when a dead person was judged in the Underworld.

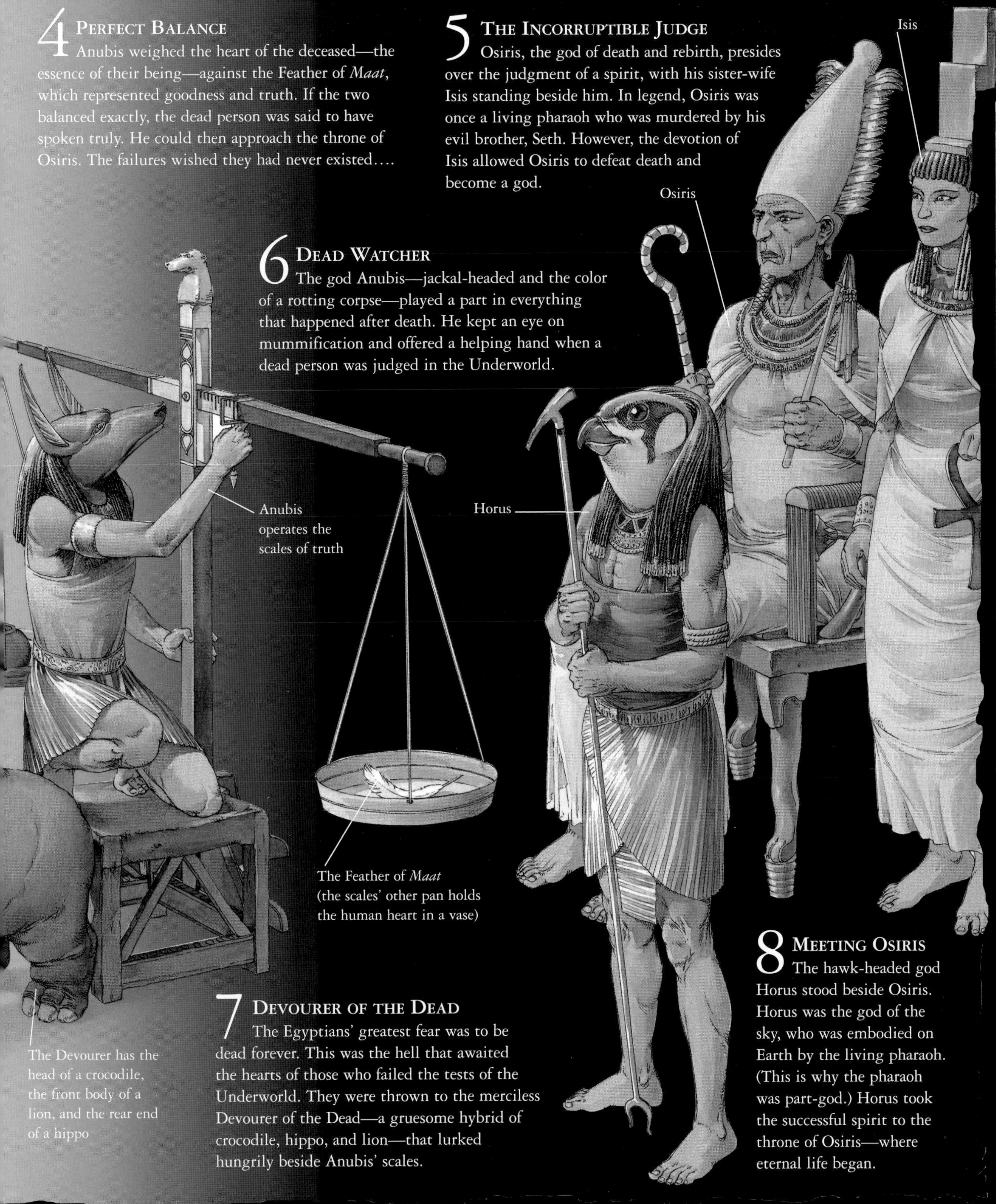

Isis
Osiris
Anubis operates the scales of truth
Horus
The Feather of *Maat* (the scales' other pan holds the human heart in a vase)
The Devourer has the head of a crocodile, the front body of a lion, and the rear end of a hippo

7 Devourer of the Dead

The Egyptians' greatest fear was to be dead forever. This was the hell that awaited the hearts of those who failed the tests of the Underworld. They were thrown to the merciless Devourer of the Dead—a gruesome hybrid of crocodile, hippo, and lion—that lurked hungrily beside Anubis' scales.

8 Meeting Osiris

The hawk-headed god Horus stood beside Osiris. Horus was the god of the sky, who was embodied on Earth by the living pharaoh. (This is why the pharaoh was part-god.) Horus took the successful spirit to the throne of Osiris—where eternal life began.

IT'S NOT SAFE....
HA! THEY'LL NEVER CATCH ME NOW!
THE OWNER OF THE BOAT EXPLAINED THAT HE HAD BEEN MENDING A LEAK!
WHAT?!
I'LL HAVE TO SWIM!
BY THE BLOODY BEAK OF MUT...?!
NOOOO!

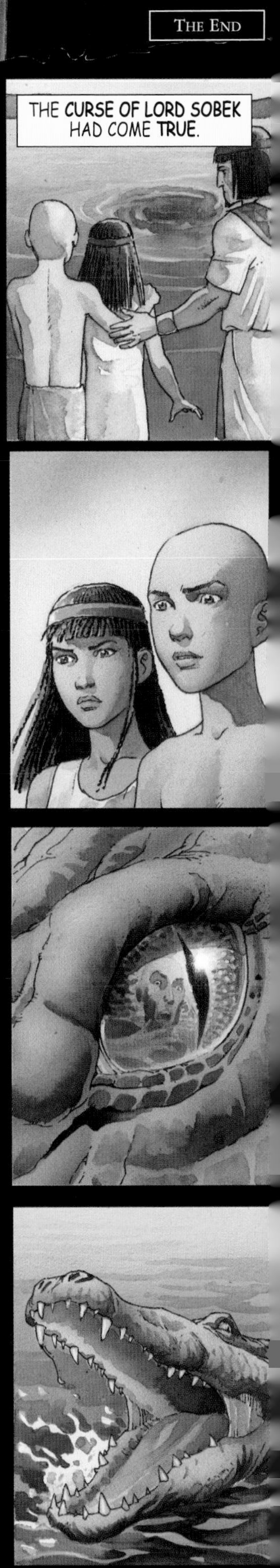

THE CURSE OF LORD SOBEK HAD COME TRUE.
THE END

Index

A

acrobats 8
afterlife 13, 14, 30-31
Amon-Ra 25
amulets 15
animals 23, 24
 see also individual names
Anubis 9, 15, 16, 31
army 9, 24
artists 28
Atum 30

B

Ba 14
Bent Pyramid, Dashur 11
Bes 30
birds 17, 23
boats 20, 21, 22-23
building 6, 20, 22
bulls 24
burial 10, 11

C

canopic jars 14, 16
cats 17
ceremonies 9, 30
clothing 5, 24, 25
coffins 10, 13, 14, 16
craftworking 28
crocodiles 4, 18, 19
Crocodilopolis 19
crowns 24

D

dancers 8
Dashur 5, 11
desert 5
Djoser, Pharaoh 10
dogs 17

E

embalming 9, 15, 16
exile 27

F

farming 8, 20, 21, 23
Fayum 5, 19
fishing 22, 23
flooding 20, 21, 30
funerals 16, 22
furniture 7, 13, 28, 29

G

games 6, 17, 29
Geb 30
gods and goddesses 4, 14, 15, 18, 19, 20, 25, 26, 28, 30-31
 see also individual names
Great Pyramid, Giza 5, 11
guards 25, 26, 27

H

Hatshepsut, Pharaoh 9
Hawara 5
hieroglyphs 4, 5, 9, 13, 14, 18, 21, 22
hippopotamuses 23
Horus 13, 30, 31
House of the Dead 16-17
hunting 23, 24

I

Imhotep 10

J

jewelry 4, 13, 14, 28, 29, 30
judges 24, 26

K

Ka 14, 15
Khufu, Pharaoh 11

L

laws 26
Libyans 25
linen 28
lions 24

M

Maat 26, 31
make-up 14, 29
marriage 9
mastaba tombs 10
Medjay 26
metals 28
mortuary temples 11
mourners 16
mummification 9, 14-15, 16-17, 31
musicians 4, 8, 25

N

Natron 15, 16, 28, 30
Nile, River 4, 5, 20-21, 22-23, 30
Nilometers 20
nobility 7
Nubia 8, 26
Nut 30

O

obelisks 18
officials 4, 8, 9, 18, 21, 25, 26, 27
Osiris 15, 31
ostriches 24

P

paints 28
palaces 7, 24-25
paper 21
papyrus reeds 21, 22, 24, 27
pharaohs 7, 8, 9, 10, 11, 12, 13, 18, 19, 24-25, 31
police force 26
priests 4, 8, 9, 11, 16, 18, 19, 26
prisoners 8, 27
punishments 27
pylons 18, 19
pyramids 4, 5, 6, 10-11, 12-13
 burial chambers 12, 13, 14
 tomb robbers 4, 11, 12, 13
 tricks and traps 12, 13

R

rituals 15, 16, 19, 25
robbers 12-13

S

scribes 4, 9, 21, 25, 26, 27
servants 4, 7, 8, 29
shops 7
shrines 11, 19
Shu 30
Sneferu, Pharaoh 11
Sobek (crocodile god) 4, 18, 19
Sobekneferu, Pharaoh 5, 6, 25, 26, 27
statues 4, 11, 18, 19, 22
Step Pyramid, Saqqara 5, 10
Syrians 24

T

Tawaret 30
taxes 21, 27
Tefnut 30
temples 4, 5, 6, 18-19
Thoth 30
tools 28
towns 6-7
trade 19, 22
transport 7, 22, 23, 24
trees 22
Tutankhamun, Pharaoh 11, 29

U

Underworld 30-31

V

Valley of the Kings 5, 11

W

wall paintings 7, 18, 19
weapons 9, 26, 28
"weighing of the heart" ceremony 30-31
writing
 see hieroglyphs

Deleted scenes

These additional panels were not used in the final story due to lack of space.

PAGE 14
Methen and Madja try their hardest to move the entrance stone.

PAGE 24
Escaping from Kenamun—and some dangerous hippos in the Nile.

PAGE 25
Lord Ini seated on his throne when the children ask for his help.

PAGE 28
Madja and Methen under armed guard in the House of the Dead.

PAGE 30
Kenamun realises the game is up and breaks away from the soldiers.

PAGE 30
Spears narrowly miss Kenamun as he runs for his life over the desert.